Ironic Life

Ironic Life

Richard J. Bernstein

polity

First published in 2016 by Polity Press

Polity Press
65 Bridge Street
Cambridge CB2 1UR, UK

Polity Press
350 Main Street
Malden, MA 02148, USA

ISBN-13: 978-1-5095-0572-2
ISBN-13: 978-1-5095-0573-9(pb)

A catalogue record for this book is available from the British Library.

Library of Congress Cataloging-in-Publication Data

Names: Bernstein, Richard J., author.
Title: Ironic life / Richard J. Bernstein.
Description: Malden, MA : Polity Press, 2016. | Includes bibliographical references and index.
Identifiers: LCCN 2015037540| ISBN 9781509505722 (hardback : alk. paper) | ISBN 9781509505739 (pbk. : alk. paper)
Subjects: LCSH: Irony.
Classification: LCC BH301.I7 B47 2016 | DDC 128–dc23 LC record available at http://lccn.loc.gov/2015037540

Typeset in 11 on 12.5 pt BaskervilleNo2BT Roman
by Toppan Best-set Premedia Limited
Printed and bound in the UK by Clays Ltd, St Ives PLC

For further information on Polity, visit our website:
politybooks.com

Contents

Acknowledgments

I want to thank my research assistant, Caecilie Varslev-Pedersen, for her meticulous assistance in preparing this book and checking the accuracy of my quotations. I also want to thank Jean van Altena. She is a superb copy editor with an exquisite sense of detail and style. And finally I want to acknowledge John Thompson, the editor of Polity, for his constant enthusiastic encouragement.

Introduction

"And by now 'irony' has been used for pretty much everything": so declares Jonathan Lear in his book *A Case for Irony* (Lear 2011: 180, n. 12). From a very different perspective, Paul de Man, in his influential article "The Concept of Irony," begins by saying that "it seems to be impossible to get hold of a definition" of irony (de Man 1996: 164). "Ironically" (we may be tempted to say), given the title of his essay, de Man informs us that irony is not a concept; consequently, it is impossible to give a stable definition of irony. Why are there these doubts about irony? If we dip into the voluminous literature that addresses irony in philosophy, rhetoric, literary theory, and cultural studies, we confront what appears to be a bottomless abyss of different, conflicting, even contradictory meanings and uses of irony.

Of course, there have been bold attempts to bring some order to this apparent chaos and to provide overviews of the different meanings, contexts, and historical uses of irony. These surveys can be useful in getting a sense of the vast terrain of "ironology." Consider such standards works as D. C. Muecke's *The Compass of Irony*, Cleanth Brooks' *The Well Wrought Urn*, Wayne C. Booth's *A Rhetoric of Irony*, Northrop Frye's *Anatomy of Criticism*, or a more recent overview, Kevin Newmark's *Irony on Occasion: From Schlegel and Kierkegaard to Derrida and de Man*. These studies are useful for specific purposes. But, except for some occasional points of overlap, one's *dominant* impression is that these authors are talking about different subjects. Their senses of what is relevant in trying to get a grip on irony differ radically. Some authors distinguish among different types of irony such as verbal, dramatic, tragic, comic, and rhetorical irony. Some insist that there are sharp differences between irony and humor. But here again, there doesn't seem to be any agreement about such classifications – or whether they obscure more than they illuminate.

Our perplexity about irony is increased when we consider it from still another perspective. Our word "irony" (and its equivalent in many European languages) is derived from the Latin *ironia*, an expression that plays a prominent role in Roman thinkers such as Cicero and Quintilian. The Latin word *ironia* is the standard translation of the Greek word *eirōneia*. (Later we will consider the problematic relation of *ironia* and *eirōneia*.) Quintilian, in early Roman times, provides a definition of *ironia* that has enjoyed a remarkable stability through the ages. He defines irony as that figure of speech or trope in which something contrary to what is said is to be understood. This formula has persisted. If you consult any contemporary dictionary, Quintilian's definition (or something very much like it) is listed as a *standard* meaning of "irony." Furthermore, whatever difficulties there may be in defining "irony," it is a word that we use all the time in everyday life – and, frequently, there isn't much difficulty in grasping how the word is being *used*. So we are confronted with the perplexity that – although "irony" *appears* to have a relatively stable use – when we examine the literature in different disciplines that deals with theoretical attempts to characterize irony and its varieties, we are faced with a chaotic babel of voices clamoring for our attention. Irony, as Lear writes, does seem to be used "for pretty much everything," and yet, at the same time, there appears to be some stability to the everyday meanings and uses of "irony." Of course, it is frequently difficult to decide whether a speech act or figure of speech in a written text is (or isn't) ironic. Some of the fiercest debates in the humanistic disciplines concern what is "truly" ironic and what is "really" intended to be ironic. This problem becomes exacerbated when we are dealing with written texts.

These preliminary remarks are intended to set the context for my own discussion of irony. A great variety of approaches to irony are viable. I admire those who have the intellectual courage and audacity to present an overview of the different approaches to irony and to explore the long history of the discussions of irony. But sometimes, something else is needed. Rather than trying to cover the territory or do justice to different approaches, it is desirable to probe in depth one vein, one line of inquiry. That is what I am doing in this study. I am acutely aware that, in doing so, I am ignoring historical periods, problematic issues, and even thinkers whom others take to be the heart of the matter. Before explaining the line of inquiry that I pursue, I want to contrast it with a different approach to the topic.

In the twentieth century, the dominant approaches to irony have been taken from the perspective of literary studies and rhetoric. When Wayne Booth published *A Rhetoric of Irony* in 1974, many literary intellectuals (especially in the United States) considered it to be the standard work on irony. Booth was writing in the shadow of the movement known as New Criticism, where irony was presumed to be the *key* concept for understanding what is *distinctive* about literary texts, especially poetry. In retrospect, it is hard to resist the conclusion that the term became so inflated that it was virtually empty. Cleanth Brooks, one of the leading proponents of New Criticism, tells us in his famous book, *The Well Wrought Urn*, that "irony" is "the most general term we have for the kind of qualification which the various elements in a context receive from the context" (Brooks 1947: 191).

Wayne Booth recognized that when irony is characterized in such a vague way, it really isn't useful. One of Booth's primary aims is to characterize irony in such a manner that it is useful for *practical* literary criticism. And he offers many concrete examples to show how we can identify irony in literary texts. Booth, although aware of theoretical discussions of irony, is not really concerned with pursuing theoretical and philosophical discussions of irony. It is against this background that one can appreciate the explosive significance of Paul de Man's famous 1977 lecture on the concept of irony (transcribed, edited, and published in his 1996 collection of essays, *Aesthetic Ideology*).

> Booth's approach to irony is eminently sensible: he starts out from a question in practical criticism, doesn't get involved in definitions or in the theory of tropes. He starts from a very reasonable question, namely: is it ironic? How do I know that the text with which I am confronted is going to be ironic or is not going to be ironic? It's very important to know that: lots of discussions turn around this and one always feels terrible when one has read a text and one is told later on that it's ironic. It is a very genuine question – whatever you have to do, it would indeed be very helpful and very desirable to know: by what markers, by what devices, by what indications or signals in the text we can decide that a text is ironic or is not. (de Man 1996: 165)

We might think that de Man is praising this "eminently sensible" approach, but he then drops a bombshell. He continues: "This supposes, of course, that such a thing can be decided, that the decision we make in saying that a text is ironic can be made, and that there are textual elements which allow you to make that decision, independently of the problems of intention which might be hidden or might not be apparent" (de Man 1996: 165–6). Booth knows that we can always ask whether a text is "really" ironic and that this can open us to an infinite regress (as Kierkegaard well understood). He indicates (in a revealing footnote) that there is a philosophical problem here, but he wants to avoid it. He says:

> The spirit of irony, if there is such a thing, cannot in itself answer such questions: Pursued to the end, an ironic temper can dissolve everything, in an infinite chain of solvents. It is not irony but the desire to understand irony that brings such a chain to a stop. And that is why a rhetoric of irony is required if we are not to be caught, as many men of our time have claimed to be caught, in an infinite regress of negations. And that is why I devote the following chapters to 'learning where to stop'. (Booth 1974: 59, n. 14)

De Man comments that this desire to understand irony, to stop and control irony, is "sensible" and "reasonable." But he goes on to argue that this is just what *cannot* be done. In this context, de Man refers to Friedrich Schlegel's main theoretical text on irony, "Über die Unverständlichkeit," which de Man translates as "On Incomprehensibility" or "On the Impossibility of Understanding." He writes:

> If indeed irony is tied with the impossibility of understanding, then Wayne Booth's project of understanding irony is doomed from the start because, if irony is of understanding, no understanding of irony will ever be able to control irony and to stop it, as he proposes to do, and if this is indeed the case that what is at stake in irony is the possibility of understanding, the possibility of reading, the readability of texts, the possibility of deciding on *a* meaning or on a multiple set of meanings or on a controlled polysemy of meanings, then we can see that irony would indeed be very dangerous. There would be in irony something very threatening, against which interpreters of literature, who have a stake in the understandability of literature, would want to put themselves on their guard – very legitimate to want, as Booth wants to stop, to stabilize, to control the trope. (de Man 1996: 166–7)

The *chasm* between Booth's and de Man's approach to irony is indicated by what each of them says about Schlegel. Booth writes: "But, fellow romantics, do not push irony too far, or you will pass from the joyful laughter of *Tristram Shandy* into Teutonic gloom. Read Schlegel" (Booth 1974: 212). In response, de Man writes: "[I]f you are interested in the problem and the theory of irony you have to take it in the German tradition. That's where the problem is worked out. You have to take it in Friedrich Schlegel (much more than August Wilhelm Schlegel), and also in Tieck, Novalis, Solger, Adam Müller, Kleist, Jean Paul, Hegel, Kierkegaard, and all the way up to Nietzsche.... But Friedrich Schlegel is the most important, where the problem really gets worked out." (de Man 1996: 167).

I do not intend to pursue de Man's "arguments" or to evaluate his striking controversial claims. De Man is, in effect, critiquing the entire approach to irony that had been characteristic of American literary critics. We might say that – if the expression had not become a cliché – that de Man was calling for a radical "paradigm shift" in dealing with irony. Everything seems to change: the problems one needs to address; how one approaches the topic of irony; the distinctions that one introduces; and the key texts and figures that one needs to confront. De Man thinks that Booth might have realized that his project was *doomed* from the start if – instead of pushing it aside – he had dealt with the treatment of irony in the German tradition, beginning with the German Romantics. Most of de Man's analysis focuses on Friedrich Schlegel, Fichte, Hegel, Kierkegaard, Nietzsche, and Benjamin. These are figures who Anglo-American literary critics had almost completely ignored. Although de Man indicates his doubts about trying to define "irony," he does finally offer a definition: "[I]rony is the permanent parabasis of the allegory of tropes. (That's the definition that I promised you – I also told you you would not be much more advanced when you got it, but there it is: irony is the permanent parabasis of the allegory of tropes.)" (de Man 1996: 179). I suspect that literary critics such as Booth and Brooks might not only find such a definition unintelligible and incomprehensible, but might scratch their heads and ask: What does this have to do with irony?

I have presented this brief sketch – this fragment – of the radical changes in approaches to irony from Brooks (New Criticism) to Booth to de Man for several reasons. First, it shows how much serious disagreement there is about irony, even if we limit ourselves to a very brief segment of the history of literary criticism and theory. This disagreement is not limited to different approaches to similar topics and problems. Rather, it isn't even clear that the signifier "irony" designates a commonly shared subject matter. Second, it does suggest a legitimate and potentially helpful way of discussing irony. One might want to investigate more carefully what the New Critics wrote about irony and try to evaluate what contribution (if any) they make to our understanding aspects of irony. Instead of claiming that Wayne Booth's project is "doomed from the start," one might try to explicate what he contributes to our understanding of "stable irony." Or if one finds de Man's critical analysis persuasive, then one might want to explore the history and the controversies generated by the German Romantics and the debates that preoccupied many nineteenth-century thinkers, including Hegel, Kierkegaard, and Nietzsche – debates that have continued into the twentieth century with Benjamin, Derrida, Foucault, and Deleuze (among others). This is the approach represented by Kevin Newmark's recent book, *Irony on Occasion: From Schlegel and Kierkegaard to Derrida and de Man*, and by Claire Colebrook's short introduction, *Irony*. Regardless of what one thinks of Paul de Man's understanding of the problem and theory of irony, he is certainly right in calling attention to the lively debates about the meaning and significance of irony by European thinkers during the nineteenth century. Many literary critics today, who have been influenced by what is called "post-modern theory" – or simply just "theory" – might expect a book on irony to deal primarily with this tradition. But as I have already indicated, this is *not* what I intend to do. So the third reason for my sketch of contemporary literary debates is to contrast it with my own project – and to explain why I am pursuing it.

Let me begin with an uncontroversial observation. Despite the lively and heated debates provoked by the German Romantics among contemporary literary theorists and rhetoricians, Anglo-American *philosophers* have not been – for the most part – concerned with irony. There is barely any interest in the topic. Indeed, there is a prevailing prejudice that the study of irony does not really belong to "serious" philosophy. Leave it to literary types! This seems strange, because virtually everyone who discusses irony, beginning with Cicero and Quintilian, takes Socrates to be the paradigmatic ironist. All too frequently, contemporary Anglophone philosophers acknowledge this and then pass on to what they take to be "serious" problems. Two significant exceptions are Richard Rorty and Jonathan Lear. Both are mavericks (I mean this as a compliment). Both are well versed in the characteristic approaches of contemporary analytic and linguistic philosophy. But both have much broader intellectual interests. Lear was trained in ancient philosophy; he is a practicing psychoanalyst, a champion of Freud, and has wide humanistic interests. Rorty was also trained in the history of philosophy, and for a time was considered to be a leading "analytic" philosopher. His interests and writings span the full range of humanistic disciplines and literature. He is at home in both Anglo-American and Continental philosophy, and has been a leading advocate of overcoming the analytic/continental divide. At a crucial stage in their philosophical careers, both of these philosophers turned to the issue of irony. Neither is particularly interested in the history of this vexed topic or with the debates taking place among the literary critics and theorists mentioned above. Neither is particularly concerned with the traditional definition of irony – saying the contrary of what one means – or with the popular view that the ironist is someone who is detached and avoids commitment. Although they sharply disagree on many philosophical issues, each approaches irony in a novel (even idiosyncratic) manner. Kierkegaard, in a famous statement, declares: "Just as philosophy begins with doubt, so also a life that may be called human begins with irony" (Kierkegaard 1989: 6). I will be returning to this pithy declaration several times throughout my book. But I cite it here because both Rorty's and Lear's views on irony can be understood as different interpretations of Kierkegaard's remark that "a life that may be called human begins with irony." Lear explicitly acknowledges the importance of Kierkegaard, and he thinks that what he is doing is elucidating an older understanding of irony that has been lost sight of in modern and contemporary discussions of irony. Rorty doesn't make any such claims about recovering what irony really means. On the contrary – as we shall see – he deliberately stipulates a new definition of irony in order to introduce the figure of the "liberal ironist." But what interests me is that, for all their differences, both of these philosophers believe that living ironically (*practicing irony*) is a key to answering the question that Socrates raises in Plato's *Republic*, a question that echoes through the ages: How should one live?

I begin my study with a presentation of Lear's understanding of ironic experience, the capacity for irony, and ironic existence. He makes some very bold and provocative claims about irony. He claims

that it is constitutive of the concepts by which we understand ourselves that they are subject to ironic disruption. Furthermore, it is
constitutive of human excellence that we develop a capacity for ironically disrupting what such excellence consists in. Human flourishing
requires cultivating a capacity for erotic ironic uncanniness. Lear
thinks of himself as recovering an older sense of irony that takes us
back to Socrates. Contemporary thinkers, he claims, have a thin,
superficial, and distorted understanding of irony. For Lear, Richard
Rorty typifies this superficial approach to irony. I think that Lear is
seriously mistaken about Rorty. Much of what Lear claims to be distinctive about irony is applicable to Rorty. I offer an interpretation of
irony in Rorty's life and work that complements Lear's reflections on
irony. Rorty shares Kierkegaard's and Nietzsche's belief that attempts
to provide *rational justifications* for our most basic convictions – what
Rorty calls our "final vocabularies" – are doomed to failure. The belief
that there are ahistorical rational justifications for our "final vocabularies" is an *illusion* that can be exorcised only by ironic therapy. After
elucidating Lear's and Rorty's conceptions of irony, I evaluate the
strengths and weaknesses of their respective views. There are serious
problems with both of their views. Despite my critical reservations, I
do think that Lear and Rorty make different, but important, contributions to a fuller understanding of the philosophical significance of
irony in living a human life.

Earlier, when I indicated the general lack of interest in irony among
Anglophone philosophers, I did not mention the one area in which
there has been a great deal of discussion of irony. The scholarly study
of ancient Greek philosophy has flourished (and continues to flourish). Anyone dealing with Socrates and Plato must confront the thorny
issue of what precisely is Socratic (and Platonic) irony. Two outstanding contemporary scholars of classical philosophy who examine the
meaning of Socratic irony are Gregory Vlastos and Alexander
Nehamas. Although they sharply disagree, they both claim that a
proper understanding of Socratic irony is fundamental for a more
general philosophical clarification of irony. The issues that Vlastos
and Nehamas raise about Socratic irony are directly relevant to the
concerns of Lear and Rorty.

But before we can even examine Socratic irony, there are preliminary problems that need to be addressed. Who is (was) Socrates? We
know that a real historical person called "Socrates" lived and died in
Athens. There are a few minimal facts about the historical Socrates

that are well established, such as the year of his death. But because Socrates never wrote anything, we do not have any *direct* evidence of what he thought and believed. All we have are reports of what he presumably said (mostly written after his death). Are these sources sufficient to reconstruct the historical Socrates? Which sources and reports can we take as reliable? These questions have been debated throughout the centuries and have never been completely resolved.

There is also a closely related issue. Socrates, of course, is the major character in Plato's dialogues. Is the Socrates portrayed in the Platonic dialogues an accurate representation of the historical Socrates? If so, which dialogues represent the historical Socrates? We will see that Vlastos and Nehamas represent two *extreme* views about the "Socratic problem." Vlastos thinks that it is, in principle, solvable – and indeed he proposes a solution. He claims that we have solid evidence whereby to reconstruct what the historical Socrates was like. He also argues that the Socrates portrayed in the "early" Platonic dialogues is a reliable portrait of the historical Socrates. Nehamas doesn't think that we will ever know what the historical Socrates was really like. Furthermore, he claims that the Socrates portrayed in the Platonic dialogues (even the so-called "early dialogues") is a "literary character" created by Plato. Plato's Socrates is a *literary fiction*.

Even if we bracket the Socratic problem and focus our attention on Plato's Socrates in the "early" dialogues, we still want to know what precisely Socratic irony is. Vlastos's answer is similar to that of Cicero and Quintilian. He calls Socratic irony "complex irony." Complex irony is the type of irony in which what is said both is and isn't what is meant. The surface content of what is said is meant to be true in one sense, but false in another sense. In his analysis of Socratic irony, Vlastos makes a fascinating claim. Although Socrates never theorized irony – that is, he never asked the question "What is F?" about irony as he does about justice, piety, virtue, etc. – Socrates actually created something radically new, he created a *new form of life*. Socrates *incarnated* in his life an irony that was free from any taint of intentional deceit. Socrates' *personality* is the basis for the Roman definition of irony – a definition that has persisted until the present day.

Nehamas disagrees with almost everything Vlastos says about Socratic irony. I have already indicated that Nehamas thinks that the Socrates of the "early" Platonic dialogues is a literary character created by Plato. He argues that Vlastos's understanding of "complex irony" is completely inadequate to capture what is distinctive about Socrates irony. Nehamas, drawing on a suggestion by Kierkegaard, characterizes Socratic irony as Socratic *silence*. Initially this seems outrageous, because Socrates is so voluble. But what Nehamas (and Kierkegaard) want to emphasize is the *opacity* of the literary character created by Plato. We can never pin down what *precisely* Socrates knows and doesn't know, what he believes and doesn't believe, what he is doing and not doing. And yet we, Socrates' successors, beginning with Plato himself, feel compelled to interpret, reinterpret, describe, and redescribe Socrates' ironic life. Nehamas claims that Socrates (the literary character created by Plato) is the origin of the tradition of philosophy as *the art of living*. This is a tradition that emphasizes the practical role of philosophy in guiding us as to how to live our lives. For all their differences, I argue that there is more in common between Vlastos and Nehamas than seems apparent initially. Nehamas's reflections on Socratic irony can be understood as developing Vlastos's tantalizing claim that Socrates created a new and unimagined form of life which he realized in himself – one for which there was no historical precedent. I show how Vlastos and Nehamas contribute new insights into what constitutes living an ironic life.

In the background of four contemporary philosophers (Lear, Rorty, Vlastos, and Nehamas) is the ghost of Kierkegaard. Lear, as I have indicated, is the most explicit in his acknowledgment of the importance of Kierkegaard for his approach to irony. His discussion of irony takes off from a single sentence from Kierkegaard's journal: "To become human does not come that easily." In a different way, Nehamas's interpretation of Socratic irony is also inspired by Kierkegaard. He takes off from what seems like Kierkegaard's paradoxical claim that the distinctive feature of Socrates is his *silence*. Although Rorty does not base his understanding of irony on Kierkegaard, it is clear that he takes Kierkegaard to be an exemplar of the ironist. We will also see that Rorty makes a sharp distinction (as does Vlastos) between Socrates the ironist as portrayed in the early Platonic dialogues and Socrates the mouthpiece for Plato's philosophy in the middle and later dialogues. Vlastos acknowledges Kierkegaard's "genius," but he thinks that Kierkegaard's treatment of Socratic irony is "hopelessly perplexed" (Vlastos 1991: 43, n. 81). (I will argue that Vlastos misunderstands Kierkegaard.)

But what, precisely, is Kierkegaard's understanding of irony? Raising the question in this manner is already misleading.

Kierkegaard uses all sorts of techniques to mask his "true beliefs" (whatever they may be), including the use of pseudonymous authors – and even writing books in which pseudonymous authors comment on other pseudonymous authors invented by Kierkegaard. He ends his famous *Concluding Unscientific Postscript* (authored by Johannes Climacus) with a "A First and Last Explanation" signed by S. Kierkegaard, in which he pleads with his readers not to ascribe the views expressed by his pseudonymous authors to him (Kierkegaard) but only to the "authors" of these books. So perhaps it is better to speak about an understanding of irony that emerges from Kierkegaard's writings (including those of his pseudonymous authors), rather than speak about Kierkegaard's understanding of irony.

Kierkegaard completed and defended his dissertation, *The Concept of Irony, with Continual Reference to Socrates*, in 1841. The dissertation consists of two parts. The first part, entitled "The Position of Socrates Viewed as Irony," treats the interpretations of Socrates by Xenophon, Plato, and Aristophanes (as well as by some of Kierkegaard's contemporaries). Part Two, "The Concept of Irony," contains a very sharp critique of Romantic irony. Throughout, Kierkegaard is at once strongly influenced by, and fiercely battling with, Hegel's understanding of Socratic irony. Despite Kierkegaard's use of the Hegelian phrase "infinite absolute negativity" to characterize Socratic irony, I show how Kierkegaard radically *swerves* away from Hegel. But *The Concept of Irony* ends with a very unsatisfactory conclusion. Kierkegaard tells us that Socrates has nothing positive to offer; he is the incarnation of infinite absolute negativity. His approach to Socrates seems so one-sided that it is difficult see how one can ever get beyond the nihilistic consequences of irony. I argue that, although Kierkegaard wants to make an extremely important point about how ironic questioning is necessary to become a "single individual," he came to realize that the discussion of Socratic irony in his dissertation was one-sided in the extreme. Indeed, Johannes Climacus explicitly says this in *Concluding Unscientific Postscript*. I then show that Climacus (and Kierkegaard) modify this view of irony to highlight the moment of *ethical passion*. This moment becomes extremely important in order to distinguish between the type of irony that is the *beginning* of becoming a self as a "single individual" and the type of irony that culminates in self-destruction. Kierkegaard's multifaceted reflections on irony enrich what we have learned from Lear, Rorty, Vlastos, and Nehamas about why a life that may be called human begins with irony. In the final chapter of my book, I integrate the insights of these thinkers and the several strands of my argument to show what we have learned about ironic life. Focusing on these four contemporary thinkers (Lear, Rorty, Vlastos, and Nehamas) and the two great ironists Kierkegaard and Socrates enables me to explore one aspect of irony in depth. I believe, however, that the issues I raise about ironic life open new approaches to the study of irony in Nietzsche, Derrida, Foucault, and Deleuze.

There is also a larger horizon for my analysis. Nehamas introduces a distinction between two different types of philosophical approach – two different traditions – that can be traced back to the Greeks. He calls these theoretical and practical philosophy. By "theoretical" (in his very broad sense) Nehamas wants to call attention to that tradition in philosophy in which the primary issue is to understand, "to get things right," to advance claims that one seeks to justify with the best possible reasons – whether these claims be about the nature of reality or the nature of knowledge, ethics, or politics. Whatever the scope of theoretical philosophy, "[w]hat philosophers study make no more claim to affecting their personal lives than the work of physicists, mathematicians, or economists is expected to affect theirs" (Nehamas 1998: 1). When evaluating the theoretical claims of philosophers (even when they are about such practical issues as ethics and politics), we want to know whether the theses advanced are correct, and we seek to evaluate the reasons offered in support of the theses advanced. Evaluating theoretical philosophical claims has nothing to do with evaluating how these philosophers live their lives.

But there is another tradition in philosophy – that was also especially prominent in the Hellenistic period whereby philosophers were primarily concerned with the art of living. In this tradition, everything – including one's theoretical reflections – is oriented to shaping how we live our lives. It is the *practice* of living that is all-important. Academic philosophy today is dominated by a theoretical orientation, so much so that many academic philosophers are not even aware of the philosophical tradition as the art of living. To the extent that they are aware of it, they view the art of living with deep suspicion. They tend, as Nehamas notes, to think of contemporaries who identify themselves with philosophy as the art of living "at best as 'poets' or literary figures, at worst as charlatans writing for precocious teenagers or, what for many amounts to the same thing, for professors of literature" (Nehamas 1998: 4). For academic philosophers working in the theoretical tradition, philosophy as the art of living sounds like those all too popular "self-help" manuals that are found on philosophy shelves in many bookstores. Throughout my inquiry, I will be concerned with the tensions between the theoretical approach to philosophy and philosophy as the art of living. I do *not* want to denigrate the importance of theoretical philosophy. But I hope to restore a sense of *balance* between these competing philosophical traditions.

Virtually all philosophers today acknowledge Socrates as an exemplar of a person who thoroughly integrated his philosophical questioning with the way in which he lived his life. And Socrates has always been the primary exemplar of the ironist. My inquiry is intended to help recover the spirit of ironic life that Socrates concretely embodies.

Chapter 1

Jonathan Lear and Richard Rorty on Irony

In the opening chapter of *The Compass of Irony*, entitled "Ironology," D. C. Muecke declares: "Getting to grips with irony seems to have something in common with gathering the mist; there is plenty to take hold of if only one could. To attempt a taxonomy of a phenomenon so nebulous that it disappears as one approaches is an even more desperate adventure" (Muecke 1969: 3). I am not sure that "nebulous mist" is the right metaphor, because even a superficial acquaintance with the history and the baffling (almost chaotic) variety of what has been described as irony might lead one to the despairing conclusion that almost anything can been labeled "irony." The volumes and articles dealing with irony would fill several libraries. There doesn't even seem to be any consensus about classifying the varieties or types of irony. Nevertheless, there are identifiable strands that run through (some of the) discussions of irony. Perhaps the most common one is that irony is a rhetorical figure of speech. Gregory Vlastos succinctly describes this strand.

> "Irony," says Quintilian, is that figure of speech or trope "in which something contrary to what is said is to be understood" (*contrarium ei quod dicitur intelligendum est*). His formula has stood the test of time. It passes intact in Dr Johnson's dictionary ("mode of speech in which the meaning is contrary to the words" [1755]), and survives virtually intact in ours: "Irony is the use of words to express something other than, and especially the opposite of, [their] literal meaning" (*Webster's*). (Vlastos 1991: 21)

If we think of irony in this way, then it is a trope that anyone can – and frequently does – use. But there isn't anything intrinsically philosophical about this use. We find it in all sorts of oral and written discourse. So we might think that describing and analyzing the variety of types of irony is primarily a subject for rhetoricians, literary theorists, or lexicographers. Recently, several philosophers have sought to recover the concept of irony, because they think it tells us something philosophically important about what it means to live a human life. They do not think of irony exclusively as a figure of speech, but as something far weightier. Although their approaches are strikingly different and they sharply disagree with each other, a common thread runs through their analyses. Irony consists of "the art of living"; it is about how we might live worthy human lives. Jonathan Lear, Richard Rorty, Gregory Vlastos, and Alexander Nehamas think it is an important task for philosophy to explicate and illuminate the meaning of irony. When we do so, we learn something fundamental about living a human life and about philosophy itself. I want to explore what each of these thinkers is telling us about irony and what I take to be the strengths and weaknesses of their respective views. In the background of their thinking stand the two great ironists in the history of philosophy, Socrates and Søren Kierkegaard. I begin by discussing Lear's and Rorty's understandings of irony (Chapter 1). Then I consider the meaning of Socratic irony, focusing on two contemporary interpretations, by Gregory Vlastos and Alexander Nehamas (Chapter 2). I take up Kierkegaard's (and his pseudonymous authors') understanding of irony as well as Socratic irony (Chapter 3). Finally, I will explore what lessons we can draw from these varying philosophical understandings of irony as they pertain to the art of living (Chapter 4).

Lear's Case for Irony

Jonathan Lear lays out his views on irony in *A Case for Irony*, based on his Tanner Lectures.[1] Lear seeks to break through "routine understandings of irony" and "routine understandings of ourselves" and "to make clear what irony is and why it matters" (Lear 2011: p. ix). From the outset he acknowledges that his sources of inspiration are Kierkegaard and Plato (more specifically, Plato's portrayal of

Socrates). For these thinkers show us that irony is fundamental to understanding the human condition. Lear tells us that Kierkegaard "has everywhere been my teacher. Socrates was his teacher. But what Kierkegaard learned from Socrates is itself a source of confusion" (Lear 2011: p. x). Lear's distinctive approach to irony takes as a point of departure a single sentence from Kierkegaard's journal, written on December 3, 1854: "To become human...does not come that easily."[2] The full entry from which this sentence is quoted reads:

> In what did Socrates' irony really lie? In expressions and turns of speech, etc.? No, such trivialities, even his virtuosity in talking ironically, such things do not make a Socrates. No, his whole existence is and was irony; whereas the entire contemporary population of farm hands and business men and so on, all those thousands, were perfectly sure of being human and knowing what it means to be a human being, Socrates was beneath them (ironically) and occupied himself with the problem – what does it mean to be a human being? He thereby expressed that actually the *Trieben* [drives] of those thousands was a hallucination, tomfoolery, a ruckus, a hubbub, busyness...Socrates doubted that one is a human being by birth; to become a human or learn what it means to be human does not come that easily." (Quoted by Lear 2011: 5)

Lear distinguishes *"the experience of irony"* from *"the capacity for irony,"* and he distinguishes both of these from what Kierkegaard calls *"ironic existence"* (Lear 2011: 9). Lear introduces several distinctions in order to explicate what he means by the experience of irony. Following Christine Korsgaard, he tells us that we constitute ourselves by our practical identities. A practical identity commits me "to norms that I must adhere to in the face of temptations and other incentives that might lead me astray" (Lear 2011: 4). Practical identities tend to be formulated as variations of social roles. Each of us has many practical identities. I am a father, a husband, a teacher, and a citizen. Normally, I acquire and occupy a practical identity unreflectively, but I may (for a variety of causes and/or reasons) reflect on what such a practical identity involves. What does a specific practical identity require me to do? What does it mean – or what ought it to mean – to be a Christian, a teacher, a citizen, or a businessman? Socrates, in Plato's *Republic*, asks Cephalus: "What is the greatest good you received by being wealthy"? Cephalus answers Socrates *reflectively* without any trace of irony. So being reflective or critical about one's practical identity does not necessarily involve irony. The reflective/nonreflective distinction does not capture the experience of irony. So what, precisely, is "the experience of irony," and how is it related to practical identity? Here we need to introduce Kierkegaard's idea of *pretense*, but not as "make-believe." He "is using 'pretend' in the older *sense* of *put oneself forward* or *make a claim*" (Lear 2011: 10). Pretense in this non-pejorative sense goes to the very heart of human agency. When I am asked – even in the simplest and most straightforward cases – what I am doing, I answer by *making a claim*. "Why are you bending down?" "I am tying my shoelaces."[3] But once we introduce this idea of pretense and distinguish it from the aspiration that is embedded in the pretense, then the gap opens for the possibility of irony.

> The possibility of irony arises when a gap opens between pretense as it is made available in a social practice and an aspiration or ideal which, on the one hand, is embedded in the pretense – indeed, which expresses what the pretense is all about – but which, on the other hand, seems to transcend the life and the social practice in which that pretense is made. The pretense seems at once to capture and miss the aspiration. (Lear 2011: 11)

The key phrase in the above passage is "the *possibility* of irony." For even when there is a gap between pretense and the aspiration embedded in the pretense, there may not yet be the experience of irony. This gap may be the occasion for non-ironic reflection on the disparity between pretense and aspiration. If I claim to be a Christian, but don't think that I need to be concerned about the poor, someone may confront me and claim that I am not a Christian because I fail to take seriously the aspiration or ideal that is embedded in the claim to be a Christian. There is a gap or disparity between pretense and aspiration. If I am challenged, I may reflect on my practical identity as a Christian, and may even reform my conduct. So where does irony come in? Consider what Lear takes to be Kierkegaard's fundamental ironic question: "In all of Christendom, is there a Christian?" or, as Lear rephrases it more bluntly, "Among all Christians, is there a Christian?" (Lear 2011: 12). "Kierkegaard," Lear tells us, "used 'Christendom' to refer to socially established institutions of Christianity, the ways in which understandings of Christianity are embedded in social rituals" (Lear 2011: 7).[4] Although on the surface the above question is similar to a tautology, we don't hear it that way. We understand that "the question asks whether amongst all who understand themselves as Christian there is anyone who is living up to the requirements of Christian life" (Lear 2011: 12). Is there a "true," "genuine," "authentic" Christian? Using the language of pretense and aspiration, we are asking whether, among those who *pretend* or make a claim to be a Christian, there is anyone who is living up to the *aspiration* embedded in this pretense. But once again, even when we interpret Kierkegaard's question in this manner, it may not provoke the experience of irony. "The ironic question on its own is neither necessary nor sufficient to generate an experience of irony" (Lear 2011: 13). To grasp the "philosophically significant sense of irony" is to focus on precisely how one *responds* to the ironic question, how it *grabs* us. Lear admits that clarifying this way of being grabbed is tricky, yet crucial, for understanding the experience of irony.

Initially, Lear distinguishes two moments of this experience. "[F]irst, there is the bringing out of a gap between pretense and pretense-transcending aspiration" (Lear 2011: 16). We have already seen that awareness of this gap is not sufficient to induce the experience of irony. It may provoke only non-ironic reflection. "Second, there is the experience of ironic uptake that, I have suggested, is a peculiar species of uncanniness" (Lear 2011: 16). Here Lear is drawing upon Freud's famous essay "The Uncanny," in which we learn that uncanniness is the experience "that something that has been familiar returns to me as strange and unfamiliar. And in its return it disrupts my world. For part of what it is to inhabit a world is to be able to locate familiar things in familiar places. Encountering strange things per se need not be world-disrupting, but coming to experience what has been familiar as utterly unfamiliar is a sign that one no longer knows one's way about" (Lear 2011: 15). This uncanniness is dramatically enhanced when what, until now, I have taken to be my practical identity strikes me as thoroughly unfamiliar. I no longer take it for granted. "Of course, the ironic question on its own does not guarantee ironic uptake – the experience of irony. But when the experience does occur, it has the structure of uncanniness" (Lear 2011: 16). The third moment that Lear specifies brings us closer to what he takes to be distinctive about the experience of irony. The experience of irony (in the paradigm case) is radically first-personal. It is not only *first-personal*, but also *present tense*. If the ironic question is to hit its target for some particular I, there must be a peculiar first-personal disruption.

To bring out what Lear is getting at, it may be helpful to consider his secular example of a practical identity – teaching. Lear describes a situation in which he is grading some papers and begins to wonder what this has to do with teaching his students. This situation may give rise to questioning the purpose of grading and to reflecting on how the activity of grading contributes to teaching. Questioning the significance of grading for my practical identity as a teacher may provoke serious reflection, but need not provoke the experience of irony. In this case, there is no ironic uptake. Such reflection and questioning is "part and parcel of inhabiting a practical identity" – the practical identity of being a reflective teacher (Lear 2011: 17). But something more extraordinary may occur – something like *vertigo*, where what seemed so familiar now seems completely unfamiliar, where I am radically uncertain about what I even mean by teaching my students, or what it means to say that I am helping them to develop. Everything that I have taken to be involved in teaching now seems wildly inadequate, and I am thoroughly shaken. My standard activities of reflection actually appear as ways of *avoiding* what I now realize the ideal calls for. It is as if an abyss has opened up between my previous understanding and what I now take to be the ideal to which I am presumably committed. "Disruption," "disorientation," "breakdown," "vertigo" – these are the expressions that Lear keeps using to characterize the experience of ironic uncanniness, where everything that was familiar now appears unfamiliar.[5]

> In the ironic moment, my *practical knowledge* is disrupted: I can no longer say in any detail what the requirements of teaching consist in; nor do I have any idea what to do next. I am also living through a breakdown in *practical intelligibility*: I can no longer make sense of myself (to myself, and thus can no longer put myself forward to others) in terms of my practical identity. (Lear 2011: 18)

This sort of disruption is a species of uncanniness, because the life I have hitherto taken to be perfectly familiar has suddenly become thoroughly unfamiliar. And I don't even know how to orient myself. But why label this "the experience of irony"? Or, to put it another way, how are we to distinguish what Lear labels "ironic disruption" from something that looks very much like it, a psychotic episode – what was once called a "nervous breakdown"? But now we come even closer to what is distinctive about ironic disruption. There is an "itch for *direction* – an experience of uncanny, enigmatic *longing*" (Lear

2011: 20, emphasis added). I am not simply frozen or incapacitated. "[I]n an ordinary experience of the uncanny, there is mere disruption, the familiar is suddenly and disruptively experienced as unfamiliar. What is peculiar to irony is that it manifests *a passion in a certain direction*" (Lear 2011: 19, emphasis added). This passion for direction is illustrated in Lear's example of the ironic uptake in response to the disruption of his identity as a teacher.

> It is because I care about teaching that I have come to a halt as a teacher. Coming to a halt in a moment of ironic uncanniness is how I manifest – in that moment – that teaching matters to me. I have a strong desire to be moving in a certain direction – that is, in the direction of becoming and being a teacher – but I lack orientation. Thus the experience of irony is an experience of *would-be-directed* uncanniness. (Lear 2011: 19)

We can begin to see the philosophical significance of Lear's phenomenological description of the experience of ironic disruption by his appeal to Platonic *Eros* as it is portrayed in the *Phaedrus*. (In the *Phaedrus* Socrates characterizes *Eros* as a species of divine madness.) "Plato emphasizes the importance of the disruptive, disorienting experience as that from which philosophical activity emerges" (Lear 2011: 20). Even if we do not accept Plato's "mythical and metaphysical interpretation" of this experience, we can nevertheless see that he is describing an experience of erotic uncanniness.

> Though Socrates [in the *Phaedrus*] is describing an intense moment of god-sent madness – and thus his language is dramatic – the structure of the experience fits the erotic uncanniness I have been trying to isolate. Those who are struck in this way "*do not know what has happened to them for lack of clear perception*" (250a–b). They are troubled by "the strangeness [*atopia*] of their condition" (251e), but they also show "contempt for all the accepted standards of propriety and good taste" – that is, for the norms of social pretense. Yet all along "they follow the scent from within themselves to the discovery of the nature of their own god" (252e–253a). (Lear 2011: 20)

Kierkegaard took inspiration from Socrates (and Lear takes inspiration from Kierkegaard), because Socrates' questioning brings out the gap between pretense and aspiration. And Socrates does this in a manner that does not simply call for reflection, but rather seeks to provoke ironic disruption. There is a standard form of the Socratic ironic question: "Among all the politicians (in Athens), is there a single politician?"; "Among all rhetoricians, is there a single rhetorician?"; "Among all the wise, is there a wise person?"[6] In each case the *possibility* of irony arises by the way in which Socrates shows "that the pretense falls short of its own aspiration. That is, a social pretense already contains a pretense-laden understanding of its aspiration, but irony facilitates a process by which the aspiration seems to break free of these bounds" (Lear 2011: 23).

Something implicit in Lear's discussion of the experience of irony needs to be made fully explicit, because it is crucial for grasping why Lear thinks that the experience of irony is so fundamental for a philosophical understanding of human life. Previously, Lear isolated three moments of the experience of irony: (1) bringing out the gap between pretense and pretense-transcending aspiration; (2) the experience of ironic uptake that is a species of uncanniness; and finally, (3), the sense in which this experience is "radically first-personal, present tense." But the first-personal experience of ironic uncanniness – unlike vertigo or a nervous breakdown – does not incapacitate us. Rather, what is peculiar to irony is that it manifests a *passion* for a certain direction. We can clarify what Lear means by returning to his example of teaching – to what happens after I have the experience of ironic disruption, when I begin to question every aspect of my being a teacher and feel completely disoriented. Because one *cares* about teaching, one comes to a halt in a moment of ironic uncanniness. Teaching matters. "[I]n the ironic experience, it is my *fidelity to teaching* that has brought my teacherly activities into question" (Lear 2011: 21, emphasis added). The experience of ironic uncanniness provokes me to start searching. Initially, this search is inchoate and indeterminate. I am thoroughly disoriented and don't know where to turn. But what am I searching for? It is the way to become a teacher – or, as we might say, a true or real teacher, not just someone who follows the normal conventions of the practical identity of teaching. If we appeal to Socrates, we are searching for a distinctive type of human excellence. "So, my ironic experience with teaching manifests an inchoate intimation that there is something valuable about teaching – something excellent as a way of being human – that isn't quite caught in contemporary social pretense or in normal forms of questioning that pretense...*It is constitutive of our life with concepts with which we understand ourselves that they are subject to ironic disruption*" (Lear 2011: 22, emphasis added).[7]

This last claim is an extremely strong one. It shows just why Lear takes irony and the experience of irony so seriously. The capacity for irony – developing the capacity to occasion an experience of irony – *is* the capacity required for achieving a distinctively *human life*. "Ironic existence is whatever it is that is involved in turning this capacity for irony into a human excellence: the capacity for deploying irony in the right way at the right time in the living of a distinctively human life" (Lear 2011: 9). It may seem from Lear's example of teaching that ironic disruption is something that *happens* to me, not something that I *actively* seek. It isn't as if I said to myself that I want to thoroughly rethink what it means to be a teacher. If that were so, I would be initiating the non-ironic activity of reflecting on what it means to be a teacher. But, according to Lear, although it may be difficult to grasp his point, we can *cultivate* the capacity for ironic disruption. One can *actively* develop a capacity for irony – "that is, a capacity for occasioning an experience of irony (in oneself and another) – into a human excellence" (Lear 2011: 30).[8] At times, Lear so emphasizes the difference between "normal" reflection about a practical identity and uncanny ironic disruption that we may fail to recognize that *both* cases involve reflection. Ironic reflection is "a peculiar form of *committed* reflection" (Lear 2011: 21). We can now better understand why Lear seizes upon Kierkegaard's phrase "To become human…does not come that easily." Turning this capacity for irony into a human excellence is what is really difficult in living a human life.

We want to get a firmer idea of what precisely is involved in ironic pretense-transcending activity. Suppose we return to the standard forms of the ironic question: "Among all Christians, is there a Christian?," or "Among all the wise, is there a wise person?" In these questions there is a first and a second occurrence of the key term: "Christian," "Christian"; "wise," "wise." For any standard form of the ironic question we can list two columns; a left-hand column and a right-hand column. The left-hand column in the above questions expresses the social pretense, whereas the second occurrence of the same term in the right-hand column invokes the aspiration embedded in the pretense. We have already noted that we can question the left-hand column – and reflectively modify what we mean – without any ironic disruption. When such questions are raised, a common (non-ironic) response is to reflect on the gap between the pretense and the aspiration. We reflect and decide what we are to do about it. So how do we tell when genuine transcendence of the right-hand column really occurs?

There are two difficulties in trying to specify what is distinctive about the transcendence that leads from the left-hand column to the right-hand column. The first is that "everything one wants to say admits of interpretation that is appropriate to the left-hand column" (Lear 2011: 26). And the second difficulty is that "what one needs to grasp is the evanescence of the right-hand column. It has all the substantiality of the Cheshire's cat smile" (Lear 2011: 26). Although Lear doesn't mention Kierkegaard's musings about indirect communication in this context, he is struggling with a similar issue. He declares: "It is as though one already has to have some capacity for irony to grasp what it is about" (Lear 2011: 26). The answer to the ironic question is not the sort of thing that can be captured by adding some further necessary or sufficient conditions – some criteria – for distinguishing the two columns. *"Everything is going to depend on how those conditions are themselves understood.* That is, one needs an ironic ear to hear the conditions in the right sort of way" (Lear 2011: 26, Lear's emphasis). It is beginning to look as if there is some sort of circularity here, because the distinctiveness of the pretense-transcending activity that Lear wants to isolate is *not* adequately captured by anything that we can *say*. Whatever we say opens itself to an interpretation that misses the point. So it seems that one must *have* the experience of irony, the peculiar type of disruptive uncanniness – an "ironic ear" – in order to capture what is distinctive about irony. This is a reason why it can be so difficult to capture what is distinctive about the uncanny disruption that provokes ironic pretense-transcending activity. If someone has never had an experience of irony, she will never grasp the deeper meaning of irony. She will be inclined, rather, to hear only the calls for further reflection on the left-hand column – adding more and more conditions and specificity. Claiming that *anything* we say about irony may be misinterpreted and fails to capture what is distinctive about the experience of irony need not lead to mystification or obfuscation. After all, there is a sense in which one may never grasp what is peculiar about love or melancholy unless one *experiences* it. Anything that we say about these experiences is open to interpretations that don't quite capture what we seek to disclose.

If *ironic existence* involves the capacity for deploying irony in the right way at the right time in living a distinctively human existence, then it demands a certain practical wisdom.

> In ironic existence, I would have the capacity both to live out my practical identity as a teacher – which includes calling it into question in standard forms of reflective criticism – *and* to call all of that questioning into question, not via another reflective question, but rather via an ironic disruption of the whole process. In this twofold movement I would both be manifesting my best understanding of what it is about teaching that makes it a human excellence *and* be giving myself a reminder that this best understanding itself contains the possibility of ironic disruption...Ironic existence thus has a claim to be a human excellence because it is a form of truthfulness. It is also a form of self-knowledge: a practical acknowledgment of the kind of knowing that is available to creatures like us. (Lear 2011: 31)

Suppose we ask the Socratic question: Can this human excellence be taught and communicated? Clearly, on the basis of what Lear has said, there are no rules, no criteria, and no specification of procedures that are *sufficient* to lead us to acquiring the capacity for ironic experience. At best, we can point to persons who *exemplify* ironic existence. We learn how to live with irony appropriately by learning from those who are already living an ironic existence. And for Lear, there are at least two notable ironists: Socrates and Kierkegaard. Of course, pointing to Socrates and Kierkegaard is helpful only if we grasp what is peculiar about them. For anything we say about them is itself open to misinterpretation. (And according to Lear, most commentators on Socrates and Kierkegaard have failed to appreciate the distinctive way in which they are ironists.) Socrates and Kierkegaard will not really speak to us as exemplars of ironists unless we already have an "ear for irony."

In describing Socrates – the exemplar of the ironist – Lear tells us that Socrates' ironic questioning seems to maintain a "weird balancing act: simultaneously (i) calling into question a practical identity (as socially understood), (ii) living that identity; (iii) declaring ignorance of what it consists in. If becoming human requires holding all of that together, no wonder Kierkegaard thinks it is not that easy to get the hang of it" (Lear 2011: 24). The first two conditions are not difficult to grasp. For the first is indicated by Socrates' practice of asking ironic questions of politicians, rhetoricians, and indeed all those who claim to know or to be wise. And the second condition is illustrated by the portrait of Socrates' character in the early Platonic dialogues – his practice of living a just, courageous, and temperate life. There is not only the negative side of Socrates' irony (which is frequently emphasized by commentators), but there is also a positive side.

> The point of Socratic irony is not simply to destroy pretenses, but to inject a certain form of not-knowing into polis life. This is his way of teaching virtue. And it shows the difficulty of becoming human: not just the arduousness of maintaining a practical identity in the face of temptation, but the difficulty of getting the hang of a certain kind of playful, disrupting existence that is as affirming as it is negating. It is constitutive of human excellence to understand – that is, to grasp practically – the limits of human understanding of such excellence. Socratic ignorance is thus an embrace of human open-endedness. (Lear 2011: 36)

Lear's characterization of irony is extremely provocative. It challenges "routine" understandings of irony. Irony is not primarily a rhetorical trope or a figure of speech. These are only derivative aspects of irony. Ironic existence, for Lear, is a human excellence. And at times he makes a much stronger claim: the claim that Kierkegaard made when he declared that "no genuinely human life is possible without irony" (Lear 2011: 37). Lear raises deep questions about what – from a philosophical perspective – it means to live a human life. We will be pursuing these questions, but first I want to enrich our canvas by examining the understanding of irony and living a human life in Richard Rorty.

Rorty on Irony, Contingency, and Liberalism

Lear concludes his first lecture on irony with two appendices. The first is entitled "Comment on Richard Rorty's Interpretation of Irony."[9] After giving a brief summary of the definition of the ironist that Rorty provides in his controversial book, *Contingency, Irony, and Solidarity*, Lear comments: "This seems to me a thin conception of irony," and it has little to do with Kierkegaard's and Socrates', (or Lear's) conception of irony. Rorty's irony is "what irony would look like if there were no right-hand resonances in life...It seems to me that Rorty's account of irony is symptomatic of something that has happened in modernity that has made it difficult to hear the resonances of the right-hand column" (Lear 2011: 38–9). I think that Lear's critique of Rorty is itself a bit "thin" – or, to be blunt

– superficial.[10] I also think that Lear fails to recognize how Rorty exemplifies many (although not all) of the key points that Lear emphasizes in his account of irony.[11] Before taking up the explicit discussion of the figure of "the ironist" and the "liberal ironist" in *Contingency, Irony, and Solidarity*, I want to examine how the life and writings of Rorty exhibit key features of the way in which Lear characterizes irony – and how this serves as a background for understanding what Rorty explicitly says about irony.

Suppose we return to Lear's illustration of teaching. Recall that Lear described how, when grading papers, he asked himself, what does grading – what does this sort of activity – have to do with teaching? Initially, this question may provoke only left-hand critical reflection. This is the sort of reflection that is (or ought to be) part of the practical identity of being a teacher. I want to be a teacher – an excellent teacher – and I question whether what I am doing is adequate to the aspiration that is embedded in the practical identity of being a teacher. Lear sharply distinguishes this left-hand reflection from the uncanny ironic disruption – something like vertigo – that occurs when I am completely disoriented, when my practical identity is thoroughly disrupted.

So how is this related to Rorty? There is plenty of evidence in both his biography and in his writings that Rorty experienced something like this uncanny disruption – the type of disruption that leads from the left-hand column to the right-hand column.[12] If we follow the course of Rorty's career as an academic philosopher, we discover that initially he aspired to be a first-rate professional philosopher. He transformed himself from a philosopher concerned with the history of philosophy and metaphilosophy into a more "respectable" analytically oriented professional.[13] We can characterize this phase of Rorty's career as one where he asked himself: What do I have to do in order to become an outstanding and well-recognized academic philosopher? – where the standards that he accepted were the prevailing criteria of the best professional philosophers. He was remarkably successful in accomplishing this when he was appointed to Princeton, one of the leading academic philosophy departments in the world. Rorty achieved the pinnacle of academic professional success when, at a relatively early age (47), he was elected president of the Eastern Division of the American Philosophical Association. (At the time of his election, he was primarily known for a few important analytic articles dealing with the mind–body problem and incorrigibility, as well as his anthology, *The Linguistic Turn*. *Philosophy and the Mirror of Nature* was published *after* he was elected president.) Rorty was among the first (and very few philosophers) to be awarded a MacArthur "genius" award. But something else was going on in his life during the 1970s. He was experiencing the type of uncanny ironic disruption that Lear describes so well. He was disoriented. What had been so familiar now became strange and unfamiliar. He began questioning what it even means to be a philosopher. He was radically questioning the very idea of philosophy as an academic discipline. We can even imaginatively formulate Rorty's ironic question: "Among all professional philosophers (in philosophy departments), is there a single philosopher?" Rorty, as he describes himself in his autobiographical essay, "Trotsky and the Wild Orchids," was making the transition from the left-hand column to the right-hand column. Rorty not only experienced this uncanny disruption, he acted on it. He resigned from Princeton and joined the faculty of the University of Virginia as a professor of humanities in 1982. And he never again joined a philosophy department.[14]

Let us pursue this transition more closely. In characterizing the experience of irony, Lear emphasizes that there is not only a disruption of one's practical identity, but also a form of loyalty to it. In Lear's example of teaching, it is the fidelity to teaching that brings his teacherly activities into question. Lear speaks of an "itch for direction" and calls this experience *"erotic uncanniness"* (Lear 2011: 20). Now for all of Rorty's critique of Philosophy with a capital "P" and what he sometimes called the Plato–Kant tradition, he was engaged in "a peculiar form of *committed* reflection" (Lear 2011: 21). We might say that Rorty was asking himself (in a right-hand column way): What does it mean to be a philosopher today? And this is a question that he continued to ask himself until the end of his life. We can see the evidence for this in the way he concludes *Philosophy and the Mirror of Nature*, when he declares: "The only point on which I would insist is that philosophers' moral concern should be with continuing the conversation of the West, rather than with insisting upon a place for the traditional problems of modern philosophy within that conversation" (Rorty 1979: 394). And in *Contingency, Irony, and Solidarity*, he writes:

> On the view of philosophy which I am offering, philosophers should not be asked for arguments against, for example, the correspondence theory of truth or the idea of the "intrinsic nature of reality." The

trouble with arguments against the use of a familiar and time-honored vocabulary is that it is expected to be phrased in that very vocabulary...Interesting philosophy is rarely an examination of the pros and cons of a thesis. Usually it is, implicitly or explicitly, a contest between an entrenched vocabulary which has become a nuisance and a half-formed new vocabulary which vaguely promises great things. (Rorty 1989: 8–9)

There are two points in this passage that I want to emphasize in relation to Lear's analysis of irony. First, it shows that when Rorty started questioning Philosophy with a capital "P," and when he began ironically critiquing what he took to be the pretensions of contemporary professional philosophers, he was *not* abandoning philosophy, but making the move – and encouraging others to do so – from a left-hand to a right-hand understanding of philosophy. For Rorty too, there was an "itch for a direction" – a type of committed reflection that is provoked by the experience of ironic disruption. Second, Rorty is basically making the point that Lear underscores when he tracks the difficulty of making this transition. When Rorty claims that the trouble with arguments against a familiar and time-honored vocabulary is that these arguments are expected to be phrased in that very *same* vocabulary, he is reinforcing Lear's point that left-hand reflection is based on the accepted canons and criteria of what counts as reflection and argument. And there is always a tendency to think that *all* reflection is some variation of left-hand reflection. Unless one has an "ear for irony," one can fail to grasp the sharp difference between these two different kinds of reflection – and thereby miss what is distinctive about the experience of irony.

If one has an "ear for irony," then one can grasp that long before the explicit discussion of irony in *Contingency, Irony, and Solidarity*, Rorty was engaging in the *practice* of irony. I don't mean that he was just making witty ironic quips. *Philosophy and the Mirror of Nature* is an exercise in irony.[15] A reader might have been alerted to this when Rorty describes the projects of Wittgenstein, Heidegger, and Dewey – if she had an "ear for irony." In his Introduction, Rorty tells us that they are the three most important philosophers of the twentieth century. Why? Because although each – in different ways – sought (in the early stages of his career) to make philosophy "foundational," they each later came to realize that these earlier projects were self-deceptive illusions. "Each of the three, in his later work, broke free of the Kantian conception of philosophy as foundational, and spent his time warning us against those very temptations to which he himself had once succumbed. Thus their later work is therapeutic rather than constructive, edifying rather than systematic, designed to make the reader question his own motives for philosophizing rather than to supply him with a new philosophical program" (Rorty 1979: 5–6).

Let us bracket the question of whether Rorty is right or wrong in the way in which he reads Wittgenstein, Heidegger, and Dewey. (Many have argued that he is mistaken.[16]) I want to focus on his practice of irony. Lear's description of the disruptive uncanniness of the ironic experience is relevant. Rorty wants to show how the accepted criteria for left-hand reflection, critique, and evaluation break down and how there is a need to make a more radical break with standard conceptions of philosophical programs. I don't think that it is accidental that he uses the expression "edifying" – which he contrasts with "systematic" – to signify this radical break. (At the time, "edifying" was the accepted English translation of Kierke-gaard's Danish *opbyggelig*.) Many analytically trained philosophers were infuriated, because throughout the first two parts of *Philosophy and the Mirror of Nature*, Rorty *seems* to be arguing like a disciplined analytic philosopher. He certainly exhibits his sophisticated knowl-edge of contemporary analytic discussions of the mind–body problem, the theory of reference, and the debates about realism and anti-realism. At times, it appears as if Rorty is using the same vocabulary in which these debates were formulated in order to advocate his own "positive" philosophical theses. But, increasingly, it becomes appar-ent that what he is really doing is undermining and deconstructing the project of analytic philosophy. This becomes clear in what Rorty takes to be the central chapter of his book, "Privileged Representa-tions," where he discusses Quine's critique of the analytic–synthetic distinction and Sellars's critique of the intuition–concept distinction. (Both distinctions are central for Kant.) Rorty claims that if we press Quine's and Sellars's critiques all the way, then the very project of analytic philosophy is undermined. "It is as if analytic philosophy could not be written without at least *one* of the two great Kantian distinctions, and as if neither Quine nor Sellars were willing to cut the last links which bind them to Russell, Carnap, and 'logic as the essence of philosophy'"(Rorty 1979: 171–2).

Rorty's target is not just recent versions of analytic philosophy, but mainstream Western systematic philosophy. Although it is impor-tant not to caricature the achievements of systematic philosophers, nevertheless, they are to be sharply distinguished from those of edifying philosophers. "Great systematic philosophers are constructive and offer arguments. Great edifying philosophers are reactive and offer satires, parodies, aphorisms" (Rorty 1979: 369).[17] Great systematic philosophers may be revolutionary insofar as they found new schools within which "normal professionalized philosophy can be practiced" – that is, left-hand argumentation and reflection. But there are also revolutionary philosophers "who dread the thought that their vocabulary should ever be institutionalized, or that their writing might be seen as commensurable with the tradition" (Rorty 1979: 369). Rorty is trying to get his readers to *experience* the rupture between left-hand philosophizing, where we are always – implicitly or explicitly – appealing to accepted standards and criteria for argumentation and the type of revolutionizing right-hand philosophizing that involves uncanny ironic disruption. And, of course, Kierkegaard is an exemplar of the edifying thinker.[18]

We can make a similar point from a slightly different perspective. One of the favorite strategies of philosophers is to claim that unless a philosophical doctrine is in accord with our basic intuitions, then we ought to reject it – or at least be dubious about it. Or, if we have conflicting philosophical intuitions, then we should try to reconcile them. The appeal to "our intuitions" is frequently the mark of entrenched forms of left-hand reflection and is used to block any transition to right-hand reflection. But Rorty suggests that "the claim that an 'adequate' philosophical doctrine must make room for our intuitions is a reactionary slogan, one which begs the question at hand" (Rorty 1989: 21). It is reactionary because it presupposes that the only legitimate type of critical reflection is left-hand reflection, where we appeal to accepted standards, criteria, and intuitions. We *do* have intuitions, but they seem to be "deep" and "basic" *because* we have been educated within intellectual traditions built around them. At times, when there is ironic disruption then the proper response should be: "so much the worse for your old intuitions; start working up some new ones" (Rorty 1997: 177).[19]

I have briefly reviewed the career and works of Rorty prior to the publication of *Contingency, Irony, and Solidarity* for two reasons. First, I want to contest Lear's view that Rorty's depiction of irony is thin because Rorty's ironist "need never leave the left-hand lane of life" (Lear 2011: 38). On the contrary, I am claiming that a proper (ironic) reading of Rorty is all about making the transition – the break

– between the left-hand and the right-hand lane. Second, by focusing on Rorty's own experience of uncanny ironic disruption, I have clarified the background for his explicit discussion of the ironist. So let us turn to this discussion.

Rorty seeks to describe and defend the figure of the "liberal ironist." In the preface to *Contingency, Irony, and Solidarity*, he gives a brief description of what he means by the "ironist" and "liberal." "I use 'ironist' to name the sort of person who faces up to the contingency of his or her own most central beliefs and desires – someone sufficiently historicist and nominalist to have abandoned the idea that those central beliefs and desires refer back to something beyond the reach of time and chance" (Rorty 1989: p. xv). As for "liberal," Rorty adopts the definition of Judith Shklar, for whom "liberals are the people who think that cruelty is the worst thing we do" (Rorty 1989: p. xv). As Rorty notes, one can certainly be an ironist without being a liberal, and furthermore, a liberal need not be an ironist. Indeed, most ironists have *not* been liberals, and most liberals have certainly *not* been ironists. It may seem that irony and liberalism are incompatible with each other. But Rorty claims that "[l]iberal ironists are people who include among these ungroundable desires their own hope that suffering will be diminished, that the humiliation of human beings by other human beings may cease" (Rorty 1989: p. xv). In chapter 4, "Private irony and liberal hope" Rorty gives his explicit definition of the "ironist."

> I shall define an ironist as someone who fulfills three conditions: (1) She has radical and continuing doubts about the final vocabulary she currently uses, because she has been impressed by other vocabularies, vocabularies taken as final by people or books she has encountered; (2) she realizes that argument phrased in her present vocabulary can neither underwrite nor dissolve these doubts; (3) insofar as she philosophizes about her situation, she does not think that her vocabulary is closer to reality than others, that it is in touch with a power not herself. Ironists who are inclined to philosophize see the choice between vocabularies as made neither within a neutral and universal metavocabulary nor by an attempt to fight one's way past appearances to the real, but simply by playing the new off against the old. (Rorty 1989: 73)

To grasp what Rorty is saying here, we need to understand what he means by a "final vocabulary."[20] Rorty claims that all human beings carry about a set of words with which they seek to "justify" their actions, beliefs, and lives. They are " 'final' in the sense that if doubt is cast on the worth of these words, their user has no noncircular argumentative recourse" (Rorty 1989: 73). When Rorty speaks of a "final vocabulary," he certainly does not mean that it rests on a firm foundation, or even that it remains constant. This is just what he is criticizing. There are all sorts of historical contingencies that influence and shape our final vocabularies. These vocabularies frequently change in the course of our life. But when doubt is cast on the worth of key words in one's final vocabulary, "their user has no noncircular argumentative recourse" by which to justify them. Rorty's main point is similar to one made by Nietzsche and Kierkegaard. They both question the very idea of a "rational justification" of our ultimate convictions.[21] We deceive ourselves (or compliment ourselves) when we think that we can rationally justify our final vocabularies. When Rorty says that the ironist "has radical and continuing doubts about the final vocabulary she is currently using," he is not making a standard epistemological point about doubt.[22] Because there is a plurality of final vocabularies – and it is always possible to create new final vocabularies – it simply makes no sense to speak as if there is one and only one final vocabulary.

Nevertheless, there is a potential danger that a single vocabulary will prevail and violently exclude all others. And in politics there is *always* the real danger of imposing a single vocabulary as "the Truth." One of Rorty's key motivations for keeping irony alive is to secure a space for creative new vocabularies – new vocabularies that can be played off against older, entrenched vocabularies. Ironists (if they philosophize) realize that there is no neutral metavocabulary to which one can appeal in making the choice between vocabularies.[23] This last claim is one of the reasons why Rorty has been charged with being a relativist (in the pejorative sense of the term), where our picture of relativism is one in which the choice of a vocabulary is completely arbitrary.[24] One must be careful here. Rorty maintains that it is an *illusion* to think that we have, or can have, some neutral standards or criteria for choosing among vocabularies. But we can play off one vocabulary against another – play off the new against the old. The force of Rorty's understanding of irony is that he is always calling into question those who think that they can do more; that they can fight their way past appearances to the real; that they can finally get things right; that they can arrive at a final vocabulary that can be, and ought to be, the vocabulary with which the world speaks to us. But "the world does not speak. Only we do. The world can, once we have programmed ourselves with a language, cause us to hold beliefs. But it cannot propose a language for us to speak. Only human beings can do that" (Rorty 1989: 6).

Rorty's critiques of any and all forms of foundationalism and representationalism are part of a master strategy for showing that it is an *illusion* to think that we can escape the contingency of the plurality of vocabularies. And irony (rather than argument) becomes a powerful way of exposing illusion. Rorty's point is similar to Kierkegaard's. In his posthumously published *The Point of View*, Kierkegaard tells us that "an illusion can never be removed directly, and basically only indirectly" (Kierkegaard 1998: 43). And from Johannes Climacus we learn that it is only with irony, humor, and satire that we can expose a deeply embedded illusion. But if it is an illusion to think that we can appeal to some ahistorical standards or criteria for comparing and evaluating competing vocabularies, then what is involved in playing off vocabularies against each other? Here, Rorty appeals to *redescription*. Ironists realize "that anything can be made to look good or bad by being redescribed" (Rorty 1989: 73).[25] Furthermore, ironists renounce the claim to formulate *criteria* of choice between final vocabularies. (This can remind us of Lear's point that there are no necessary and sufficient *criteria* for specifying what constitutes irony.) We play off vocabularies against each other by an appeal to metaphors, stories, and narratives. If we are seeking to show why an entrenched vocabulary should be abandoned in favor of a new one, we use a variety of rhetorical devices to make the new vocabulary as attractive as possible. We don't do this solely by argument (in any standard sense of argument), because insofar as the standards of what constitutes a "good argument" are themselves dependent on an entrenched vocabulary, the appeal to argument is question-begging. When Rorty says that ironists are "never quite able to take themselves seriously," he means that they are aware that the terms in which they describe themselves are always subject to change. They are "always aware of the contingency and fragility of their final vocabularies" (Rorty 1989: 73–4). Rorty is an ironist who is *passionately* committed to a liberal project of diminishing human cruelty and humiliation. "For liberal ironists, there is no answer to the question 'Why not be cruel?' – no noncircular theoretical backup for the belief that cruelty is horrible" (Rorty 1989: p. xv).

I want to relate what Rorty is suggesting to my earlier comments about ironic disruption. I have stressed Rorty's radical questioning of analytic philosophy – and, more generally, systematic philosophy. Using Lear's terminology, Rorty is challenging the entrenched standards and criteria of what constitutes good and clear argumentative philosophy – left-hand philosophical reflection – the accepted norms of the philosophical profession (including the accepted ways of revising these norms). But he isn't doing this in order to *argue* for better standards and criteria. He seeks, ironically, to disrupt this demand for neutral standards and criteria. In place of a picture that held – and still holds – many philosophers captive, he is elaborating (redescribing) an alternative picture whereby we are liberated from the grip of thinking that the *only* type of legitimate philosophical reflection is left-hand reflection. This is what Rorty, following Thomas Kuhn, calls "normal" puzzle-solving philosophizing. He is trying to get us to see – or better, to *experience* – the constriction and limitations of this way of thinking. He wants to keep open the space for more radical right-hand ways of imagining and thinking. He seeks to keep open human possibilities: that is, new, creative ways of shaping ourselves and establishing solidarity with our fellow human beings. Irony, then, is *not* merely a rhetorical trope (although Rorty is a master of the ironic quip), but rather a proposal for how *we* – or *some of us* – might live our lives.

Thus far, I have been approaching Rorty's conception and use of irony from the perspective of Lear – especially Lear's analysis of the ironic disruption in moving from left-hand reflection to right-hand questioning. Lear claims that, given Rorty's understanding of irony, "all that remains is irony as a form of detachment" (Lear 2011: 39). But this misses Rorty's primary point. It is not some sort of detachment that he advocates, but rather a *commitment* to the liberal project of diminishing cruelty and humiliation. "Ironically," Rorty's multifaceted attack on the very idea of ahistorical neutral epistemological standards is intended to expose the illusion of neutral detachment. But there are also striking differences between Lear and Rorty on irony. Rorty would never say – as Lear does – that he is going "to make clear what irony is" or that irony is revealed "by a grasp of what should matter when it comes to living a distinctively human life" (Lear 2011: p. ix). For Rorty, this way of speaking smacks of the essentialism and "getting things right" that he relentlessly criticizes. Rorty doesn't claim, as Lear does, to tell us what irony "really is," but rather *redescribes* a way of thinking about the ironist. This indicates another major difference between Lear and Rorty. Rorty pushes his contingency theme all the way. For him, there is no underlying essence or deep structure to language or the self.

The difference between Rorty and Lear is also reflected in the different ways in which they read and use Freud. Citing Freud's essay on Leonardo da Vinci, Rorty seeks to support his thesis about the contingency of the self; that "we are all too ready to forget that in fact everything to do with our life is chance, from our origin out of the meeting of spermatozoon and ovum onwards...Every one of us human beings corresponds to one of the countless experiments in which these 'ragioni' of nature force their way into experience" (Rorty 1989: 31). Summing up Freud's contribution, Rorty writes:

> [P]oetic, artistic, philosophical, scientific, or political progress results from the accidental coincidence of private obsession with a public need. Strong poetry, commonsense morality, revolutionary morality, normal science, revolutionary science, and the sort of fantasy which is intelligible to only one person, are all, from a Freudian point of view, different ways of dealing with blind impresses – or more precisely, ways of dealing with different blind impresses: impresses which may be unique to an individual or common to the members of some historically conditioned community. None of these strategies is privileged over others in the sense of expressing human nature better. No such strategy is more or less human than any other. (Rorty 1989: 37–8)[26]

This is not Lear's Freud. Lear, who is both a philosopher and a practicing psychoanalyst, thinks that Freud presents us with a far more determinate structure of the human psyche. Lear argues that "unconscious fantasy can function as something like an unconscious practical identity" (Lear 2011: 57), and that in the course of psychoanalytic therapy a clash between unconscious and conscious practical identities may emerge. The experience of ironic disruption plays a vital role in psychoanalytic therapy. Analysts help analysands to verbalize their core unconscious fantasies – their unconscious practical identities. "This is a process that *cannot* occur without ironic disruption" (Lear 2011: 59, emphasis added). For Lear, there is an "important form of psychic integration that consists in deploying well a capacity for ironic disruption. A deep form of integration can occur only when we find creative ways to disrupt and disturb ourselves" (Lear 2011: 66).[27] Rorty would, of course, raise doubts about any talk of a "deep form of integration" of the self, but he might well endorse Lear's call for "creative ways to disrupt and disturb ourselves."[28]

How does Rorty's understanding of irony relate to Kierkegaard and Socrates? Unlike Lear, Rorty does not draw explicitly on these two ironists when he introduces his explicit characterization of irony. But they are both in the background of his thinking. We have already noted that, according to Rorty, Kierkegaard is an exemplar of the edifying thinker – the thinker who offers "satires, parodies, aphorisms" to undermine the prevailing prejudices about systematic philosophy. Kierkegaard uses irony to disrupt. And his disrupting power is achieved not by argumentation, but by metaphors, narratives, and redescriptions – what Kierkegaard's pseudonymous character Johannes Climacus calls "indirect communication." Concerning Socrates – the Socrates of the Platonic dialogues – everything depends on how we interpret what Socrates is doing. If Socrates is taken to be the mouthpiece for Plato's metaphysical and epistemological doctrines, then Rorty, of course, rejects this sort of Platonism.

But there is another (Rortian) way of interpreting Socratic irony and his profession of ignorance. Socrates, the gadfly, has cultivated an art by which he is able to question the beliefs of his interlocutors. He is constantly questioning conventional "wisdom." As for Socratic ignorance, Rorty interprets this as an acknowledgment that Socrates is aware that he does *not* have final answers to the questions that he raises. More radically – in Rorty's terms – Socrates "knows" that there is no "noncircular argumentative recourse" for answering his questions. This is why so many of the early Platonic Socratic dialogues end in aporias. And yet Socrates (as portrayed by Plato) leads a virtuous life. Leading such a life does *not* require knowing the answer to the question: What is virtue? This is the key to understanding Socrates' ignorance as a form of wisdom. It is not a type of ignorance, which we must wait for Platonic knowledge to rectify, but rather an ignorance that calls into question the very possibility of such knowledge. Rorty might well agree with Lear's claim about Socratic irony that I have already cited: "The point of Socratic irony is not simply to destroy pretenses, but to inject a certain form of not-knowing into polis life" (Lear 2011: 36). But for Rorty this "not-knowing" calls into question the *pretense* that we can break out of our vocabularies and know reality as it really is. Rorty's ironic intention is to pierce through the crust of philosophical convention and to encourage the transition to a liberal utopia in which there is both playful self-creation and the furthering of a human solidarity that diminishes cruelty (Rorty 1979: 13).

Some Questions Concerning Lear and Rorty

I have presented sympathetic accounts of Lear's and Rorty's reflections on irony – and why they think irony is philosophically important for living a human life. I now want to stand back and raise some critical questions about their respective views on irony. We need to realize just how radical a departure Lear is making from what he labels "routine" understandings of irony – so radical that he opens himself up to the charge that he is simply changing the subject. When Cicero introduced the Latin word *ironia*, he wrote: "Urbane is the dissimulation when what you say is quite other than what you understand... In this irony and dissimulation Socrates, in my opinion, far excelled all others in charm and humanity. Most elegant is this form and seasoned in seriousness."[29] Whether one agrees or disagrees with Cicero, he is clearly referring to what one (and Socrates in particular) *says*. Irony presumably has something to do with a special use of language. But for Lear, irony has (essentially) nothing to do with language. He emphasizes the non-verbal uncanny experience of disruption. Recall his description of the ironic experience when one radically questions oneself as a teacher. "I am *struck* by teaching in a way that disrupts my normal self-understanding of what it is to teach (which includes normal reflection on teaching)" (Lear 2011: 17). Why call this the experience of irony?[30] At best, according to Lear, the linguistic expression of irony is only a derivative form of irony. It is never quite clear how such a use of language is derived from the non-linguistic uncanny experience of disruption. In order to have the experience of irony, there must be an awareness of the disparity between the pretense and the pretense-transcending aspiration. Furthermore, the awareness of this disparity may provoke only non-ironic left-hand reflection. There also needs to be a first-personal present tense ironic uptake. The individual undergoing this experience need not *verbalize* this. Even if one agrees with Lear that "this little disrupter is crucial to the human condition" (Lear 2011: p. ix), Lear's reasons for claiming that this is what irony "really is" aren't clear. Lear stresses that the experience of irony is first-personal present tense. An individual who undergoes ironic disruption engages in right-hand "committed reflection."

This entire process need not involve any communication with another person. But irony as a *figure of speech* (whether spoken or written) is typically addressed to another person (or to some audience). In *this sense* irony is dialogical. But Lear's analysis of irony is *essentially monological* (first-personal). How, then, do we derive the dialogical forms of ironic discourse from the monological experience of irony? It may be thought that this experience of irony arises in response to such ironic questions as "Among all Christians, is there a Christian? Or, "Among all the wise, is there a wise person?" But the individual who undergoes the experience of irony need not (as Lear indicates) be asking herself questions that take this form. An ironic question is neither a necessary nor a sufficient condition for the disruptive experience of irony; it all depends on how it "grabs" us. There is something troubling about this radically subjective way of characterizing irony. We might ask the Socratic question: How are we to distinguish the "real thing" from a "false coin"? How are we to tell that there really has been an experience of irony? After all, Lear himself insists that we can't specify determinate criteria or necessary and sufficient conditions for the experience of irony. And even if one makes a sincere first-personal report that one is experiencing ironic disruption, one can presumably be mistaken about what one is actually experiencing. This issue becomes even more troubling when we are dealing with a written text and not a direct oral report. We can see this in the way Lear interprets Socratic irony as portrayed in the Platonic dialogues. In the Platonic dialogues, we are given minimal *direct* information about Socrates' "radically first-personal" experiences – even when Socrates is being described by other interlocutors. Lear, on the contrary, thinks that Plato *does* tell us what Socrates is experiencing.

I want to examine closely one of Lear's examples. For it reveals the ingenuity of Lear's attempt to show that Socrates undergoes an uncanny disruptive ironic experience. Despite Lear's ingenuity, I believe his interpretation is extremely problematic and unpersuasive. Lear quotes a famous passage from the *Symposium* in which Alcibiades describes Socrates' behavior at the battle of Potidaea.

> One day, at dawn, he started thinking about some problem or other; he just stood outside trying to figure it out. He couldn't resolve it, but

he wouldn't give up. He simply stood there, glued to the same spot. By midday many soldiers had seen him, and, quite mystified, they told everyone that Socrates had been standing there all day, thinking about something. He was still there when evening came, and after dinner some Ionians moved their bedding outside, where it was cooler and more comfortable (all this took place in the summer), but mainly in order to watch if Socrates was going to stay out there all night. And so he did; he stood on the very same spot until dawn! He only left the next morning, when the sun came out, and he made his prayers to the new day. (*Symposium* 200c–d)[31]

In this passage (as well as in the rest of the *Symposium*) Plato does not *explicitly* say anything about what Socrates was experiencing when he stood still throughout the night. Strictly speaking – assuming that Alcibiades gives a truthful account (as he insists he does) – we don't have any independent evidence to support Alcibiades' belief that Socrates was thinking about "some problem or other." All we really know is that Socrates stood glued to the same spot throughout the night.[32] But Lear doesn't hesitate to declare that "Socrates is standing still not because he is too busy thinking, but because he *cannot walk*, not knowing what his next step should be. I take this to be a moment of erotic uncanniness: *longing* to move in the right direction, but not knowing what that direction is" (Lear 2011: 34, Lear's emphasis). Presumably Alcibiades "just doesn't get it" – but Lear does. It begins to look as if Lear is projecting his interpretation of what Socrates *must* be experiencing, rather than sticking to the information provided by the text. In her commentary on Lear, Christine Korsgaard accuses Lear of rewriting Alcibiades' account of Socrates at Potidaea. She writes "I think Alcibiades is right here and that Lear is wrong. To me, the arresting thing about Socrates is his utter self-possession. He is always so completely himself, in any circumstance: in battle, while being tried by the Athenians for his life, on the day of his death" (in Lear 2011: 82). But when Lear defends his interpretation, he creates further problems for himself. He agrees that what Alcibiades says is true. "Socrates *is* thinking about *a* problem, but Alcibiades completely misses what that truth is. This is, I think, an instance of Platonic irony: there is a meaning of Alcibiades' utterance that transcends the particular meaning that Alcibiades intends. Alas, most interpreters, Korsgaard included, stick with Alcibiades' own understanding of his words – his pretense – and they thereby miss the irony" (Lear 2011: 84–5). If Socrates comes to a halt simply because he is absorbed in thinking about a problem, then his coming to a halt would be utterly contingent; it would lack philosophical significance.

> Socrates coming to a halt is a necessary outcome and manifestation of the situation he is in...If Socrates is aware that he does not yet know what his next step should be, then practically speaking, he *cannot* take a next step. Standing still is the form that his knowing that he does not know takes. In this interpretation, standing still is not just a contingent fact about eccentric Socrates; it is the practical manifestation of his understanding of his own ignorance. It is a form of self-knowledge. (Lear 2011: 85)

Lear thinks that his interpretation of this incident is more elegant and more philosophically illuminating than Alcibiades' "flat-footed" interpretation, and more illuminating than Korsgaard's – and that of virtually all other interpreters of the *Symposium* – who presumably miss the point of Plato's irony.[33] But I don't think that Lear's interpretation is more "elegant." It strikes me as both forced and convoluted. For Lear makes all sorts of tacit presuppositions without clarifying or justifying them. He speaks here of Platonic rather than Socratic irony. And although it is clear that he wants to distinguish Platonic from Socratic irony, he never really explains what the difference is. Lear also presupposes that Socrates coming to a halt is *either* utterly contingent *or* practically necessary. And if it is contingent, "[i]t would have no philosophical significance." Why not? And why this *either/or*? For all the ingenuity of Lear's interpretation, there doesn't seem to be any textual evidence in the *Symposium* to support the dubious claim that Socrates' standing still all night "is a form of self-knowledge," or that Socrates cannot move because he doesn't know what his next step should be. According to Lear, Socrates is experiencing ironic disruption; he is thinking solely about himself; he can't (necessarily) take the next step. All this is supposed to be a manifestation of Socratic ignorance and Socratic self-knowledge. Again, if we ask how Lear *knows* all this, or if we ask for the textual basis for his making these controversial claims, it appears to come down to Lear's claim that he (and perhaps he alone) *grasps* Plato's irony. Even though Socrates remained completely silent, and neither he, nor Plato, ever explicitly say what Socrates was thinking when he stood alone through the night, Lear has no hesitancy in asserting that Socrates is undergoing the experience of irony. This is one more reason for claiming that, according to Lear, the experience of irony has nothing to do with what one does or does not say.

Earlier, I underscored Lear's claim that one has to have an "ear for irony." The distinction between non-ironic left-hand questioning and ironic right-hand questioning cannot be determined by piling up necessary and sufficient conditions. One "needs an ironic ear to hear the conditions in the right sort of way" (Lear 2011: 26). Even if we acknowledge the need for "an ironic ear," Lear doesn't face up to the hard issue as to how such an appeal can be abused. What are the signs (if any) that one really has a *genuine* "ear for irony" – that one hears correctly? How do we know (even in a fallible way) that someone who claims to really "get it" does indeed get it. It almost seems as if Lear has decided what irony "really is" and then invented a dubious interpretation of Socrates' standing still at Potidaea to fit his subjective understanding of the experience of irony.[34]

One of the crucial steps in Lear's overall argument is to move from the *experience of irony* to a *capacity for irony*. "Developing the capacity for irony," Lear tells us, "is developing the capacity to occasion an experience of irony (in oneself or in another)" (Lear 2011: 9). He also declares that ironic disruption is not only something that happens to us, but something that we can *actively* cultivate. Acquiring the capacity for irony requires that we actively (and not just passively) develop the capacity to occasion an experience of irony. It is hard to see how this works, especially in light of the sharp distinction between left-hand and right-hand questioning. I can *actively* engage in self-critical reflection – left-hand reflection. Returning to the example of teaching, it is part of my practical identity as a teacher to engage in such reflection. But can I actively will to have an uncanny ironical disruption of my practical identity? Can I will to experience something like the vertigo that I experience when all bets are off and I am completely disoriented, when I don't know what my next step should be? Can I actively will a breakdown in practical intelligibility? There is something deeply paradoxical here. On the one hand, Lear consistently stresses the break between left-hand and right-hand reflection. The more he stresses that I can *actively* develop a capacity for irony, the more it appears that I can deliberately and reflectively (left-hand reflection) induce the occasion of the experience of irony in myself and perhaps in others. But then it seems that there is *continuity* (not a radical break) between left-hand and ironic right-hand reflection. Using Lear's example of teaching, we may ask: What do I have to do (what can I do) to bring about the type of uncanny disorienting first-personal experience that makes me call into question *all* my previous understanding of teaching? *Either* (like vertigo) the experience of irony is something that *happens* to me *or* by deliberate *active left-hand* questioning I can induce the experience of irony in myself (and perhaps in others).

A primary reason why Lear makes the case for irony is because it is essential for understanding *human excellence*. He begins his lecture by affirming that "being human is thus linked to a conception of human excellence" (Lear 2011: 3). Although this has been a familiar theme in philosophy since the time of the ancient Greeks, Lear (following Kierkegaard) seeks to make this familiar theme uncannily unfamiliar. He concludes his lecture by returning to the lessons appropriated from the two great ironists Socrates and Kierkegaard. Earlier I cited Lear's claims about how Socrates injects a form of not-knowing into polis life. Here is the full passage:

> The point of Socratic irony is not simply to destroy pretenses, but to inject a certain form of not-knowing into polis life. This is his way of teaching virtue. And it shows the difficulty of becoming human: not just the arduousness of maintaining a practical identity in the face of temptation, but the difficulty of getting the hang of a certain kind of playful, disrupting existence that is as affirming as it is negating. It is constitutive of human excellence to understand – that is, to grasp practically – the limits of human understanding of such excellence, Socratic ignorance is thus an embrace of human openendedness. (Lear 2011: 36)[35]

Concerning Kierkegaard, Lear writes:

> Kierkegaard says that "no genuinely human life is possible without irony." On the interpretation I have been developing this would mean: It is constitutive of human excellence that one can develop a capacity for appropriately disrupting one's understanding of what such excellence consists in. Human flourishing would then partially consist in cultivating an experience of oneself as uncanny, out of joint. This is what it would mean to get the hang of it, the erotic uncanniness of human existence. (Lear 2011: 37)

What precisely does Lear mean by "human excellence"? I believe there are deep problems here that Lear passes over all too facilely. In his teaching example, he tells us that "it is my *fidelity* to teaching that has brought my teacherly activities into question" (Lear 2011: 21). Developing a capacity for ironic disruption "is not merely a disruption of one's practical identity; it is a form of loyalty to it. So, my ironic experience with teaching manifests an inchoate intimation that there is something valuable about teaching – *something excellent as a way of being human* – that isn't quite caught in contemporary social pretense or in normal forms of questioning that pretense" (Lear 2011: 22, emphasis added). But there is a fundamental ambiguity in the phrase "something excellent as a way of being human." We normally think that there is something valuable about teaching, and that being an excellent teacher is one way of being an excellent human being. Suppose we change the example and think of the practical identity of being an executioner, a torturer, or a mobster like Tony Soprano. In each of these social roles there is a set of conventions and normal practices associated with it. Let us also suppose that an individual experiences ironic disruption of one of these practical identities (as some of the episodes of the *Sopranos* suggest about Tony Soprano). He may have the experience of complete disorientation or disruption, and he may even experience an inchoate sense of direction whereby he seeks to become a "real" or better killer or mobster. After all, when Lear initially introduces the idea of pretense and social role, he doesn't tell us or indicate how we are to evaluate different practical identities – such as being a teacher, a mobster, a sniper, or a warrior.[36] Each may have its own *internal form of excellence*. Ironic disruption may well help someone to perfect his practical identity as a mobster, just as it may perfect someone else's practical identity as a teacher. We can distinguish the pretense (the claim to be a teacher or a mobster) from the aspiration or ideal which is embedded in each of these social roles. There are torturers, killers, and mobsters who bungle their roles, and there are those who perform them excellently. Lear slips from (a) the idea of performing a practical identity excellently to (b) being an excellent human being. It is a *non sequitur* to claim that if someone performs a practical identity or social role excellently, then he is an excellent human being. One can well imagine that the teacher in Lear's example who experiences the uncanny ironic disruptive experience about his teaching turns out to be a morally horrible human being. Consequently, a crucial step is missing from Lear's overall argument – the gap between fulfilling a practical identity excellently *and* becoming an excellent human being. Lear doesn't provide any basis for ranking or evaluating different practical identities and their distinctive excellences. Nor does he explain the relation between performing a practical identity excellently and being an excellent human being.[37]

There is a further problem concerning fulfilling a practical identity excellently. Many practical identities are culturally dependent. To perform a social role excellently requires an elaborate interlocking set of cultural practices. In *Radical Hope*, Lear gives a thick description of what is involved in being an excellent Crow warrior – an excellent Crow human being. Lear then graphically describes the way in which this culture was destroyed when the Crows were forcibly restricted to living on a reservation. In such a catastrophe (for the Crows) it no longer makes any sense to speak of the type of *human excellence* that the Crows were able to achieve *before* the catastrophe. Because the cultural conditions for achieving human excellence can change radically, we need an account of what constitutes human excellence that is independent of culturally constituted – or socially constructed – practical identities.

Lear claims that Socratic irony is a way of teaching virtue. But many of Socrates' interlocutors turn out to be tyrants or rogues. There isn't a single *unambiguous* example in which Socrates actually succeeds in injecting the form of not-knowing that Lear describes – the type of ignorance that leads to a change in *how they live their lives*. Of course, Socrates occasionally gets his interlocutors to admit that they are mistaken on some specific claim. (For example, Agathon admits that he is mistaken about the character of *Eros* in the brief dialogue that Socrates has with him in the *Symposium*.)

But there is an even more troubling question that may be raised. Consider a person (call her Jane) who never experiences ironic disruption, but who is thoroughly admirable because she engages in serious left-handed reflection and constantly works toward achieving the pretense-transcending aspiration embedded in her practical identity as a teacher. She is a teacher who is always critically reflecting on her performance and successfully improving it. Compare her with Sally, who experiences the uncanny ironic disruption that Lear describes, but never achieves the excellence that Jane does as a teacher. Why should we privilege Sally, who experiences uncanny ironic disruption? What is the basis for claiming that no "genuinely human life" is possible without irony? Why is Sally somehow more genuinely human than Jane (who never has undergone the experience of irony)? Getting the hang of developing strenuous left-handed reflection may be no less difficult than getting the hang of right-hand committed reflection. And isn't Jane's achievement as a teacher a form of human excellence? Or, to make the contrast even more dramatic, imagine that Sally is a teacher who has experienced uncanny ironic disruption. But she is so consumed with self-doubt that she never quite gets her act together despite her search for direction. She never again achieves the excellence she achieved before she was ironically disoriented. What we need – and I fail to see that Lear has provided it – is an *independent argument* to show that (a) to achieve human excellence, we must experience irony; and (b) that no genuinely human life is possible without irony.[38]

I have raised a number of difficulties concerning Lear's case for irony. I think these are serious problems that need to be confronted. He fails to clarify the difference between achieving a practical identity excellently and being an excellent human being. He does not really provide an adequate account of what constitutes human excellence – or why irony is *essential* for achieving a distinctively human life. Nevertheless, Lear describes an important phenomenon (however we label it) that philosophers have frequently neglected, and which deserves to be recognized. Something like the uncanny disruptive experience that provokes a search for a new direction *does* occur in human life. And one can also welcome Lear's emphasis on the need to break routines (what Rorty, using Dewey's expression, calls "shattering the crust of philosophical convention"). Lear is particularly sensitive to the fact that much of what we call reflection (left-hand reflection) follows established conventions and practices. He is calling for a more imaginative and radical questioning of our conventional practical identities. He appropriates Kierkegaard in order to show why becoming human does not come that easily, and he stresses how getting the hang of it is at once difficult and treacherous. We may be skeptical about Lear's claim that he is showing us what irony "really is." But Lear does elucidate *a* (not *the*) way of thinking that reveals the philosophical significance of irony for living a human life.[39]

Unlike Lear, Rorty doesn't claim to tell us what irony "really is." On the contrary, he strongly objects to such essentialist claims. He makes it perfectly clear that he is *stipulating* what he defines as "irony" and the "ironist." For all Rorty's idiosyncratic playfulness, his purpose is a serious one. He wants to foster a liberal utopia, and he realizes that one can no longer justify liberal convictions by grounding them in something more fundamental. According to Rorty, it is "metaphysicans" who believe that their final vocabularies and their liberal convictions can be rationally grounded and secured.[40] In this sense, Rorty is clearly post-metaphysical, and he thinks that contemporary liberals have to face up to this. Ever since *Philosophy and the Mirror of Nature* (and even before) Rorty has been a consistent critic of epistemology and its successor disciplines. He views the theory of knowledge, epistemology, as a desire for confrontation and constraint. It proceeds on "the assumption that all contributions to a given discourse are commensurable." By "commensurable" Rorty means "able to be brought under a set of rules which will tell us how rational agreement can be reached on what would settle the issue on every point where statements seem to conflict" (Rorty 1979: 316).

He boldly contrasts epistemology with hermeneutics, where "hermeneutics is an expression of hope that the cultural space left by the demise of epistemology will not be filled" (Rorty 1979: 315). In his later writings, Rorty drops the contrast between hermeneutics and epistemology, but he never relented in his critique of epistemology and representationalism. I mention this because it is "ironic" that his characterization of the ironist is infected with epistemological terminology. And this has led to a great deal of confusion and criticism – and even to self-criticism.[41] This epistemological point of view is indicated when Rorty tells us that the ironist has "radical and continuing *doubts* about the final vocabulary she currently uses" and that "she realizes that *argument* phrased in her present vocabulary can neither underwrite nor dissolve these doubts" (Rorty 1989: 73, emphasis added). The words "doubt" and "argument" are classic epistemological expressions. I want to sort out what is misleading and what is insightful in Rorty's description of irony. If we think of doubt in the way that Descartes uses the expression in his *Meditations* – or even in the way that Peirce speaks of inquiry as a movement from doubt to belief – we find little in common with what Rorty intends. He certainly is not advocating some sort of epistemological skepticism, practice of methodical doubt, or even a new Peircean way of thinking about inquiry. Frankly, I don't think that Rorty ever had any *genuine* "radical and continuing doubts" about his liberal convictions. From his youth to the end of his life, Rorty consistently advocated progressive liberal views. Nevertheless, when he speaks about doubts, he wants to make an important philosophical point. He is claiming that our "final vocabularies" cannot be grounded on some sort of foundation. More generally, they cannot be "rationally justified" – when this is taken to mean justified on the basis of unassailable or even "reasonable" premises. We might label this Rorty's Nietzschean point, because, as mentioned previously, Nietzsche constantly sought to expose the *illusion* of a "rational justification" of our cherished values and convictions. Rorty is not simply confessing that he cannot justify *his* "final vocabulary." He has a much stronger thesis: philosophers (especially those indebted to the Plato–Kant canon) are under the *illusion* that the "true" final vocabulary can be rationally justified – and that providing such a justification is one of the primary aims of philosophy. Rorty is in basic agreement with Wittgenstein (as well as with Kierkegaard, Nietzsche, Freud, and Lear) that a form of therapy is sometimes required to "exorcise" our most cherished philosophical illusions. Those who accuse Rorty of being a relativist are explicitly or implicitly assuming that we do have rational criteria for evaluating competing final vocabularies. This is precisely what Rorty calls into question. If we want to defend a final vocabulary, then we do this by making it as attractive as possible for a specific audience. The language of relativism is parasitic on the language of absolutism. Rorty thinks that we should drop (not try to refute) the vocabulary of relativism, absolutism, and rational justification. To put Rorty's point in the most favorable light, we might say that philosophers who think that they can give some sort of knock-down argument to justify a final vocabulary are deluding themselves. What they are actually doing (when unmasked) is seeking to make *their* final vocabularies as attractive as possible.

Instead of describing the ironist as "having radical and continuing doubts" (which misleadingly suggests some sort of existential angst), Rorty would have been clearer – and prevented misunderstanding – if he had simply said that the ironist knows that her final vocabulary is the result of all sorts of historical contingencies, and that other contingencies generate other final vocabularies. She knows that it is an illusion to think that her vocabulary or any other final vocabulary can be rationally justified (in a noncircular manner) or is somehow closer to reality. Furthermore, we are not merely passive recipients of these vocabularies; we are free to create new vocabularies. And it is this creative freedom that Rorty wants to foster.[42]

But what does Rorty mean when he declares that all we can do is play off vocabularies against each other? What does it mean to make a vocabulary look attractive? We need to unpack Rorty's claims that

(a) there is "no noncircular *argumentative* recourse" for justifying a final vocabulary; and (b) that if the ironist philosophizes, she is aware "that *argument* phrased in her present vocabulary can neither underwrite nor dissolve" her doubts (Rorty 1989: 73, emphasis added). This raises a larger and more fundamental issue, one that underlies Rorty's entire approach to irony: the contrast that he draws between *redescription* and *argument*. Once again, Rorty misleads the reader about some of his most important insights.

Rorty is a complex thinker, but there are at least two major strands in his thinking. There is what I have called the "reasonable Rorty" (with whom I mostly agree), and there is the "outrageous Rorty," who deliberately provokes and infuriates his readers. Rorty frequently introduces all sorts of provocative distinctions (and then frequently abandons them in subsequent writings). The distinction between epistemology and hermeneutics plays an important role in the concluding sections of *Philosophy and the Mirror of Nature*, but is dropped in subsequent writings. In *Contingency, Irony, and Solidarity*, Rorty introduces what strikes many as an idiosyncratic distinction between private and public life. Both hostile and sympathetic critics (including myself) have raised all sorts of objections to the way in which Rorty draws and uses this distinction.[43] The fundamental dichotomy in *Contingency, Irony, and Solidarity* is the dichotomy between *argument* and *redescription*. Rorty tells us that he is not going to argue but propose a redescription. "Conforming to my own precepts, I am not going to offer arguments against the vocabulary I want to replace. Instead, I am going to make the vocabulary I favor look attractive by showing how it may be used to describe a variety of topics" (Rorty 1989: 9). Many philosophers have been outraged by such remarks – and simply dismiss Rorty as not "serious." Most philosophers, whatever their orientations, firmly believe that argument is the life blood of philosophy. Every significant philosopher has offered *some* arguments (good or bad) to support the theses they advance. So to say "I am not going to offer arguments" is taken to mean that I do not propose to do philosophy (full stop). Furthermore, to suggest that argument is always to be understood as internal to a given contingent vocabulary certainly looks like "bad relativism."[44]

I don't want to pursue these lines of attack here. Rather, I want to show that there is something wrong and deeply misleading about the way in which Rorty draws the distinction between *argument* and *redescription*. This distinction actually obscures what he means by irony.

Let us consider how Rorty understands "argument." I believe that his characterization of argument comes close to a caricature of philosophical argument. At times, Rorty suggests that an argument consists of premises and a conclusion where there are clear rules for determining whether the argument is valid or not – the sort of thing that one learns in an elementary logic class. Or, to put the point in a more sophisticated form, we may say that an argument consists of premises and a conclusion where there is a clear decision procedure – an algorithm – by which we can determine whether it is valid or not. Clearly there are arguments like this – even complex arguments – and we may even need a sophisticated computer program to evaluate such arguments.

Let us reconsider Rorty's characterization of "commensurable" in *Philosophy and the Mirror of Nature*, because this is the way in which he thinks about philosophical argument. Here again is his definition of "commensurable": "By 'commensurable' I mean able to be brought under a set of rules which will tell us how rational agreement can be reached on what would settle the issue on every point where statements seem to conflict. These rules tell us how to construct an ideal situation, in which all residual disagreements will be seen to be 'noncognitive' or merely verbal, or else merely temporary – capable of being resolved by doing something further" (Rorty 1979: 316).

Now, whatever lip service is paid to such an idea of commensurability and algorithmic decision procedures, this has little to do with the actual activity of presenting, defending, and criticizing arguments in *real* philosophical discourse. Most of the time philosophers argue with each other without clear decision procedures. Frequently, they can't even agree on what constitutes a good or a bad argument. And sometimes there is little agreement about what actually are the precise arguments to be evaluated. This is not a criticism of philosophical argumentation, but a *description* of what actually goes on when philosophers argue with each other.

Consider some examples from the history of philosophy. Philosophers are still debating what, precisely, are Plato's arguments supporting his "theory of forms" and what are Aristotle's arguments justifying his conception of universals and particulars. Volumes have been written about what, precisely, are Kant's arguments in his Transcendental Deduction, or what (if any) are the arguments that Hegel employs to support his claims about Absolute Knowing. Even if we restrict ourselves to some of the classics in analytic philosophy, such as Quine's arguments about the analytic–synthetic distinction or Sellars's arguments for "psychological nominalism," there are serious disputes about what, precisely, these arguments are, and whether they are good or bad arguments. My point is that real argument in philosophy is rarely (if ever) anything like what Rorty characterizes as argument. Sometimes the most difficult issue is to figure out what the arguments are before we can evaluate them. The very idea of a "philosophical argument" is what once was called "an essentially contested concept." And the appeal to argument is frequently abused: for example, when certain hard-core analytic or linguistic philosophers claim that there is no need to take Continental philosophers seriously because they don't even know how to argue.

Let us turn to "redescription," and in particular to Rorty's claim that he will not offer arguments, but rather give a redescription. Frankly, I find this claim (and others in a similar vein) disingenuous. *Contingency, Irony, and Solidarity* is filled with arguments to support controversial theses. He *argues* that there is no essence to language or the self; that "only sentences can be true" (Rorty 1989: 9); that a concern for solidarity should replace the obsession with objectivity; that there is "no standpoint outside the particular historically conditioned and temporary vocabulary we are presently using from which to judge this vocabulary" (Rorty 1989: 48). These are extremely controversial theses. Moreover, Rorty offers a whole battery of arguments and reasons to support his theses. He is operating – despite his denials – in what Sellars calls the "logical space of reasons." Rorty is arguing all the time. Indeed, he is a *master* of the argumentative style of philosophizing, which is illustrated by his responses to his critics in *Rorty and his Critics* (Brandom 2000). Rorty is even responsive to critical arguments when he is persuaded that the critic has exposed some mistake in his views.[45] (Of course, it still has to be determined whether Rorty's arguments are *good* or *bad*.) In sum, I am claiming that Rorty not only offers a caricature of argument (insofar as he thinks that there are clear rules for determining what is an argument), but that he is also *mis-describing* his own sense of redescription insofar as he suggests that it doesn't involve arguments. Rorty's sharp contrast between argument and redescription doesn't hold up. *Real philosophical argument is much less "algorithmic" than Rorty suggests, and redescription involves far more argumentation that Rorty indicates.* To use Rorty's jargon, we may say that the boundary between argument and description is a "fuzzy" one; there is far more continuity between argument and redescription in Rorty's own work (and indeed in that of many other philosophers) than he indicates.

It may seem that my critique of Rorty's distinction between argument and redescription is a digression from our concern with his understanding of irony. But in fact it brings us closer to the central issues about irony. There are different styles of argumentation in philosophy, and they change in the course of history (just as they do in scientific discourse), and it is also true that some of those thinkers whom we include in the philosophical canon, like Plato and Nietzsche, employ myths, narratives, genealogies, metaphors, satires, parodies, and a great variety of other rhetorical devices to persuade us to adopt their views. Virtually all philosophers use metaphors (and other figures of speech) in developing their philosophical positions. And these figures of speech are *constitutive* of their philosophical argumentation. A great deal of the power of what Descartes claims in his *Meditations* is conveyed by his metaphors. Lest one think that this metaphorical language has been eliminated from analytic philosophy, one need turn only (for example) to the writings of Carnap, Quine, Sellars, McDowell, and Brandom.

We can characterize Rorty's ironic stance negatively and positively. On the negative side, we learn that the dream of philosophers to find some ultimate foundation for their final vocabularies is a misguided illusion. There is no such foundation (or at least, we have *good reasons* to doubt that there is such a foundation). The idea that there are permanent ahistorical standards to which we can appeal in evaluating competing final vocabularies is untenable. The idea that we can advance transcendental arguments that are truly universal and necessary (and can withstand any historical contingency) is a hopeless project. The idea that we can break out of our vocabularies and somehow know reality and the world directly is a misguided fiction.

On the positive side, the practical wisdom of Rorty's ironist is that she is convinced by these claims. She is aware of the complex historical contingencies that have formed her final vocabulary, and she also knows that there are alternative final vocabularies. Rorty's ironist would endorse what Isaiah Berlin says about Joseph Schumpeter.

Berlin ended his essay ["Two Concepts of Liberty"] by quoting Joseph Schumpeter, who said, "To realise the relative validity of one's convictions and yet stand for them unflinchingly, is what distinguishes a civilized man from a barbarian." Berlin comments, "To demand more than this is perhaps a deep and incurable metaphysical need; but to allow it to determine one's practice is a symptom of an equally deep, and more dangerous, moral and political immaturity." In the jargon I have been developing, Schumpeter's claim that this is the mark of the civilized person translates into the claim that the liberal societies of our century have produced more and more people who are able to recognize the contingency of the vocabulary in which they state their highest hopes – the contingency of their own consciences – and yet have remained faithful to those consciences. (Rorty 1989: 46)

I want to integrate the strands of my discussion of Rorty's ironist. I have suggested that Rorty's "epistemological" characterization of the ironist is misleading. I am referring to his talk of "radical doubts" and "noncircular argumentative recourse." I also think that the basic dichotomy between *redescription* and *argument* will not stand up to criticism. Nevertheless, I do think that Rorty is showing us something extremely important about irony and about its relevance for philosophy and human life. He is telling us that if we are completely honest, we must realize that it is an illusion to think we can (even in principle) come up with definitive ahistorical "rational justifications" to support our final vocabularies. All we can do is to try to make our preferred vocabularies as attractive as possible. And we do this by a combination of redescription and argument. Some philosophers manage to achieve this balance in a way that opens up new ways of thinking. Rorty's ironist, at her best, wants to liberate us from the dead weight of past vocabularies and open up space for the imaginative creation of new vocabularies. Giving up on the idea of "rational justification," realizing that our vocabularies are ungroundable, that they arise from historical contingencies, need (and should) not lead to epistemological skepticism, relativism, or cynicism. Again, all these "isms" are parasitic on the illusory expectation that we can achieve more in philosophy – that we can achieve some ultimate grounding, that there are rational justifications that stand outside historical time.[46] (This is what Dewey once called "the quest for certainty" – and he advocated that we give up this quest.) For Rorty's liberal ironist, there may be no definitive answer to the question "Why not be cruel?" – "no noncircular theoretical backup for the belief that cruelty is horrible" (Rorty 1989: p. xv). The key words here are "noncircular *theoretical* backup." This is just another way of saying that we cannot provide a definitive rational justification that supports this version of liberalism. But the liberal ironist can – and this is what Rorty actually tries to do – support her liberal convictions by making them as attractive as possible. And Rorty does this with an imaginative combination of argument and redescription. The epigram for Rorty's liberal ironist (and Rorty himself) might well be Schumpeter's remark: "to realise the relative validity of one's convictions and yet stand for them unflinchingly, is what distinguishes a civilized man from a barbarian" (Rorty 1989: 46).[47]

Chapter 2

What is Socratic Irony?

In the background of Lear's and Rorty's conceptions of irony stand the two great ironists Socrates and Kierkegaard. This is explicitly acknowledged by Lear and is implicit in Rorty's redescription of irony, but they interpret Socrates and Kierkegaard differently. For Lear, the first philosopher (in the history of Western philosophy) to exemplify the experience of right-hand, uncanny ironic disruption was Socrates – the Socrates portrayed in the Platonic dialogues. Rorty, on the other hand, focuses on Socrates as gadfly, as questioner – the figure engaged in unending conversation with his fellow human beings (who Rorty sharply distinguishes from the "Socrates" who is the ventriloquist for Plato's metaphysical and epistemological views). In his 1979 presidential address to the American Philosophical Association, Rorty defends the idea that one can be a pragmatist without "abandoning one's loyalty to Socrates" (Rorty 1982: 171). But suppose we ask the question: What exactly is Socratic irony? For all the apparent direct simplicity of this question, answering it involves confronting all sorts of issues that have been hotly debated throughout the ages – and are still being debated. For example, who are we speaking about when we refer to Socrates? Is it the actual human being who lived and died in Athens in 399 BC? Or are we speaking about the Socrates portrayed by others, such as Aristophanes, Xenophon, Plato, and Aristotle? Can we reconstruct what Socrates was really like on the basis of the reports that we have about him? We also need to face the seeming paradox that Socrates – who is considered by many to be the most

important figure in the history of philosophy – never wrote anything.[1]
All we have are reports about what he said and did by his contempo-
raries and his successors. Establishing who it is that we are calling
Socrates is only the beginning of the complex task of dealing with
Socratic irony.

The Greek word *eirōneia* is most frequently translated as "irony" in
English. But what is the meaning of *eirōneia* in Attic Greek? Does
eirōneia have the same semantic range of connotations and associa-
tions as the English word "irony"? When Cicero and Quintilian introduced the Latin word *ironia* to translate the Greek *eirōneia*, were they
introducing a new interpretation of irony? These are just some of the
key issues that must be raised before one even gets to the question:
What is Socratic irony? The literature on these and related issues is
vast. I will give a brief overview of what is involved in these scholarly
debates. I want to focus on two classical scholars who have widely
contrasting answers to our question: Gregory Vlastos and Alexander
Nehamas.

Vlastos is recognized as one of the most distinguished twentieth-
century scholars of Greek philosophy. He is known for his striking
interpretations of the Platonic dialogues, and also for training many
scholars who themselves have had distinguished careers. Throughout
his life, he was fascinated by the figure of Socrates. Shortly before his
death he published *Socrates: Ironist and Moral Philosopher*, the culmina-
tion of more than forty years of thinking and writing about Plato and
Socrates. Vlastos touches on most of the issues that I have raised
above about Socrates and irony. So I want to use Vlastos's reflections
as a starting point for dealing with these debates, before examining
his own controversial interpretation of Socratic irony. Vlastos does
believe that we can reconstruct the *historical* Socrates – the real person
who lived and died in Athens.[2] He also argues that if we read the early
Platonic dialogues correctly, they present an accurate portrait of the
historical Socrates. In this respect, Vlastos fits within a long tradition
going back centuries wherein it has been maintained that the Socratic
problem – the problem of discovering who the historical Socrates was
– can be solved. Furthermore, Vlastos thinks that he has solved it.
(Of course, he admits his own fallibility and characterizes his solution
as a hypothesis – but one for which he argues vigorously.) Vlastos
makes a sharp distinction between the portrayal of Socrates in Plato's
early dialogues and the portrayal in the middle dialogues. He refers
to these as Socrates$_E$ and Socrates$_M$. Vlastos divides the Platonic

dialogues into three groups: "early," "middle," and "late."[3] He makes the strong claim there is an *"irreconcilable difference between Socrates_E and Socrates_M."* In short, there isn't one Socrates in the Platonic dialogues, there are *two* Socrates. Vlastos spells out his hypothesis by listing ten theses, "each of which specifies in its part A a trait of Socrates_E exhibited *only* in (one or more) dialogues in Group I, and in its part B a trait of Socrates_M exhibited *only* in (one or more dialogues) in Group II."[4] Consequently, Vlastos thinks we can discern the real *historical* Socrates from a correct reading of Plato's early dialogues. Actually his hypothesis is a bit more subtle than this.

> On my hypothesis, Plato's overriding concern, in stark contrast to Xenophon's professed aim in his Socratic writings, is not to preserve memories of Socratic philosophizing, but to create it anew – to bring it alive in dramas whose protagonist philosophizes *more Socratico*. That remembered material should be used copiously is only to be expected. But my hypothesis does not bank on that. For what it proposes is that Plato in those early works of his, sharing Socrates' basic philosophic convictions, sets out to think through for himself their central affirmations, denials, and reasoned suspensions of belief by pitting them in elenctic encounter against the views voiced by a variety of interlocutors. In doing this Plato is producing, not reproducing, Socratic philosophizing. Employing a literary medium which allows Socrates to speak for himself, Plato makes him say whatever *he* – Plato – thinks *at the time of writing* would be the most reasonable thing for Socrates to be saying just then in expounding and defending his own philosophy. (Vlastos 1991: 50)

Vlastos does not rely exclusively on his interpretation of Socrates_E to establish his hypothesis. He realizes that discriminating between two different "Socrates" in the Platonic dialogues is *not* sufficient to establish that the portrait of Socrates in the early dialogues is the *historical* Socrates. But he argues that Aristotle and Xenophon confirm his historical hypothesis (at least in respect to his first four theses).[5] Vlastos's views are controversial – and indeed his claims about the two antithetical portraits of Socrates in Plato's dialogues have generated a great deal of controversy. Despite the originality of Vlastos's interpretation, he actually belongs within the tradition of Plato interpretation that stresses the changes and development that take place from early to middle to late Platonic dialogues. This way of reading the Platonic dialogues has been vigorously criticized by those who reject this developmental approach to Plato. One of the most distinguished contemporary classical scholars who challenges Vlastos and presents an alternative reading of the early and middle dialogues is Charles Kahn. Kahn not only rejects Vlastos's claims about the two irreconcilable portraits of Socrates in the Platonic dialogues, he also rejects all varieties of developmental views that suggest that a chronological reading of the dialogues shows how Plato's views developed. He contrasts a developmental approach with a unitarian approach that stresses the unity of Plato's thought.[6]

> For it is only from the moral and metaphysical standpoint defined by the *Phaedo* and *Republic* that we can properly understand Plato's philosophical intention in composing such dialogues as the *Laches*, *Charmides*, *Euthyphro*, and *Protagoras*. Such is the central thesis of this book. My interpretation is to this extent unitarian, in that I contend that behind the literary fluctuations of Plato's work stands a stable world view defined by his commitment to an otherworldly metaphysics and to the strict Socratic moral ideal (Kahn 1996: pp. xv–xvi)

Consequently, Kahn rejects the developmental claim that there is a distinctive Socratic period in Plato's work. He also brings out the literary significance of the dialogue form. He explores the background of Plato's Socratic dialogues by examining the genre of Socratic dialogues that preceded Plato. Kahn argues that the genre of Socratic dialogues is a genre of literary fiction – not a vehicle for representing the actual historical Socrates. Plato's dialogues are themselves literary fictions.[7] Furthermore, Kahn criticizes those who think that we can reconstruct the views of the historical Socrates on the basis of Xenophon's and Aristotle's comments. Kahn supports his claims and interpretation in meticulous detail. He sees the indirect and gradual mode of exposition in the early dialogues as Plato's artistic device to prepare his readers for his new and radically unfamiliar view of reality.

I have rehearsed the opposing views of Vlastos and Kahn to indicate just how controversial the Socratic problem is. Of course, what is most impressive about both Vlastos and Kahn is the nuanced detail with which they argue for, and support, their conflicting interpretations with analyses of individual dialogues. Frankly, although I am not a classical scholar, I find Kahn's interpretation (for the most part) far more persuasive and philosophically congenial than Vlastos's. I especially appreciate the way in which Kahn is sensitive to the literary form of the dialogues, and how it contributes to the meaning of the content of the dialogues. But let us turn to Vlastos's answer to the question: What is Socratic irony?

Gregory Vlastos: Socratic Irony as Complex Irony

Regardless of how one resolves the issue of whether we can extract a historical Socrates from the early Platonic dialogues or whether we stress the artistry of Plato in creating the figure of Socrates, we still have to face the issue of the meaning of irony. Here we find another tangled problem. Ever since Cicero and Quintilian first discussed *ironia*, it has become almost conventional to speak about Socratic irony (and to translate *eirōneia* as "irony"). But there is the thorny philological issue of what *eirōneia* (and its cognates) mean in Attic Greek. Once again, we can begin with Vlastos's acute observations. In contrast to our modern understanding of irony, Vlastos informs us that "when we go back to the Greeks [we] discover that the intention to deceive, so alien to our word for irony, is the normal in its Greek ancestor *eirōneia, eirōn, eirōneuomai*" (Vlastos 1991: 23).[8] Plato uses the expression with this meaning in the *Republic* when Thrasymachus, in his famous outburst, speaks of "Socrates' customary *eirōneia*." "Thrasymachus is charging that Socrates lies in saying that he has no answer of his own to the question he is putting to others: he most certainly has" (Vlastos 1991: 24). According to Thrasymachus, Socrates is deceiving his interlocutors. In this context, Vlastos asserts that there is "no excuse for rendering *eirōneia* here by 'irony'" (Vlastos 1991: 25). But if a standard meaning of *eirōneia* in Attic Greek is the "intent to deceive," then how do we get to our more modern sense of irony, which involves mockery and ridicule, but *not* intentional deception. Vlastos notes that very occasionally *eirōneia* is used to mean mockery rather than willful deception in Attic Greek. This provides the background for Vlastos's positive understanding of Socratic irony.[9]

The question then, for Vlastos, is how did *eirōneia* – with its *primary* connotation of the willful deception – become *ironia* ("irony"). To explain this change, Vlastos refers to an analogous phenomenon related to the word "pretend." The primary sense of "pretend" involves deception – for example, when a con man pretends to have high connections or a malingerer pretends to be sick. But there is a secondary sense of "pretend," which is innocent of deception, as when we say that a child pretends that her color chips are money.[10] Vlastos draws an analogy between these two senses of "pretend" (a primary and a secondary sense) and two senses of *"eirōneia."*

> What happened, I suggest, is this: when [*eirōneia*] gained currency in Attic use (by the last third of the fifth century at the latest), its semantic field was as wide as that of "pretending" in present-day English and *eirōn* had strongly unfavorable connotations – was used as a term of denigration or abuse – because the first of those two uses predominated heavily over the second; to be called an *eirōn* would be uncomplimentary at best, insulting at worst. But turn the pages of history some three hundred years – go from Greece in the fourth century BC to Rome in the first – and you will find a change which would be startling if long familiarity had not inured us to it. The word has now lost its disagreeable overtones. When Cicero, who loves to make transliterated Greek enrich his mother tongue, produces in his fashion the new Latin word, *ironia*, the import has an altogether different tone. Laundered and deodorized, it now betokens the height of urbanity, elegance, and good taste…And [with] Quintilian, two generations later, consolidating Cicero's use of the term…we are no longer in any doubt that *ironia* has shed completely its disreputable past, has already become what it will come to be in the languages and sensibility of modern Europe: speech used to express a meaning that runs contrary to what is said – the perfect medium for mockery innocent of deceit. Subsidiary in the use of the parent word in classical Greece, this now becomes the standard use. *Eirōneia* has metastasized into irony. (Vlastos 1991: 28)

We lack the "massive linguistic data" to explain exactly what made this happen, but we can say *who* made it happen: Socrates.

> [Socrates] changes the word not by theorizing about it but by creating something new for it to mean: *a new form of life realized in himself* which was the very incarnation of [*eirōneia*] in that second of its contemporary uses, as innocent of deceit as is a child's feigning that the play chips are money, as free from shamming as are honest games, though, unlike games, serious in its mockery (*cum gravitate salsum*), dead earnest in its playfulness (*severe ludens*), a previously unknown, unimagined type of personality, so arresting to his contemporaries and so memorable for ever after, that the time would come, centuries after his death, when educated people would hardly be able to think of *ironia* without its bringing Socrates to mind. And as this happened the meaning of the word altered. The image of Socrates as the paradigmatic *eirōn* effected a change in the previous connotation of the word. Through

the eventual influence of the after-image of its Socratic incarnation, the use which had been marginal in the classical period became its central, its normal and normative use: *eirōneia* became *ironia*. (Vlastos 1991: 29, emphasis added)

Vlastos claims that Socrates created *a new form of life*.[11] Consequently, Socrates effects a change in the meaning of irony by *exemplifying* a new type of *personality* that was unknown or even unimagined before him. In this respect, Vlastos agrees with Lear and Rorty that irony is not only a figure of speech, but is philosophically important for grasping a distinctive form of human life. (We will see the importance of this central claim when we consider Nehamas's critique of Vlastos.) Vlastos introduces the term "complex irony" to characterize what is distinctive about Socratic irony.

Here we see a new form of irony, unprecedented in Greek literature to my knowledge, which is peculiarly Socratic. For want of a better name, I shall call it "complex irony" to contrast it with [simple irony]. In "simple" irony what is said just isn't meant: taken in its ordinary, commonly understood, sense, the statement is simply false. In "complex" irony what is said both is and isn't what is meant: its surface content is what is meant to be true in one sense, false in another. (Vlastos 1991: 31)

To explain and support his claim about Socrates, Vlastos presents an interpretation of Alcibiades' speech in the *Symposium*. (Unlike Lear, who focuses on Alcibiades' report of Socrates' behavior at Potidaea, Vlastos treats another part of the speech.) For Vlastos, the key sentence in the speech is "He [Socrates] spends his entire life *eirōneuomenos* and jesting with people" (*Symposium* 216E4, quoted by Vlastos 1991: 33). How are we to read *eirōneuomenos* in this passage? "When Quintilian...remarks that *ironia* may characterize not just a text or a speech but 'an entire life' (*vita universa*) Socrates is his only example. So we know how he would have read *eirōneuomenos* in the text" (Vlastos 1991: 33). Vlastos claims that if we follow Quintilian we shall understand that Socrates is a lifelong ironist, and not a lifelong deceiver. For Vlastos, irony in general – and Socratic irony in particular – emphatically does *not* involve willful deception. To nail down his point, Vlastos refers to several other parts of Alcibiades' speech in which cognates and variants of *eirōneia* are used, including the following passage:

He heard me out. Then, most *eirōnikōs*, in his extremely characteristic and habitual manner, he said: "Dear Alcibiades it looks as though you are not stupid (*phaulos*), if what you say about me is true and there really is some power which could make you a better man: you must be seeing something inconceivably beautiful in me, enormously superior to your good looks. If that is what you see and you want to exchange beauty for beauty, you mean to take a huge advantage of me: you are trying to get true beauty in exchange for seeming beauty – 'gold for brass'. (*Symposium* 218D6–219A1, quoted in Vlastos 1991: 36)

And Vlastos comments: "Here, I submit, it is incontestably clear that 'ironically' *has* to be the sense of *eirōnikōs*, for the context gives no foothold to the notion of pretence or deceit" (Vlastos 1991: 36). Socrates (at least as portrayed by Plato) is credited with effecting this transformation. Vlastos remarks that one of Socrates' chief claims to fame is to be the first to exemplify true irony. This "contribution to the sensibility of Western Europe" is "no less memorable an achievement than is his contribution to our moral philosophy" (Vlastos 1991: 43).[12]

Vlastos's interpretation of Socratic irony is impressive. He combines enormous erudition and sensitivity to Greek texts with an ability to write clearly (and informally) about extremely complex and controversial issues. In his Introduction, he declares: "This book is for readers of Plato's earlier dialogues who have felt [Socrates'] strangeness, have asked themselves what to make of it, have pondered answers to its enigmas... What I offer should not distract them from their encounter with the Socrates who lives in Plato's text. It should take them back there for a closer look" (Vlastos 1991: 1). One reader who did take a closer look – at once an admirer and a sharp critic of Vlastos – is Alexander Nehamas, Vlastos's former student.

Before proceeding, I want to call attention to a perplexity that lies at the heart of Vlastos's discussion of Socratic irony and will serve as a transition to Nehamas's very different approach. On the one hand, as I have noted, Vlastos claims that Socrates created a new form of life, a previously unknown, unimagined type of personality. Yet, when we actually turn to what Vlastos says about irony, it is hard to see what all the fuss is about. Socratic irony is a form of complex irony. "In 'complex' irony what is said is and isn't what is meant: its surface content is meant to be true in one sense, false in another" (Vlastos 1991: 31). There is nothing exceptional about complex irony. When

Vlastos sums up his thesis that "what irony means is simply expressing what we mean by saying something contrary to it," he tells us that
this is "something we do all the time – even children do it – and if
we choose to do it we forfeit in that very choice the option of speaking
deceitfully" (Vlastos 1991: 43). So even if we accept Vlastos's claim
that Plato's Socrates was the first to exhibit complex irony, it is hard
to see how this justifies "the large claim" that Socrates created a new
form of life. It is easy to come up with trivial examples of complex
irony, but Vlastos seems to have more in mind when he claims that
Socrates is the paradigmatic ironist. Indeed, he does. He has in mind
the "great philosophical paradoxes of which we hear in Plato's earlier
dialogues, like Socrates' disavowal of knowledge and teaching. Each
of these is intelligible only as a complex irony" (Vlastos 1991: 32).[13]
This commits Vlastos to the claim that there is a *sense* in which
Socrates *does not know* and *does not teach* and another sense in which he
does know and *does teach*. But, at the very least, it is contestable (and
has been contested) whether we can precisely define the sense in
which Socrates knows (and does not know) and the precise sense in
which he teaches (and does not teach). I mention these problems here
(which I will discuss later in more detail in Chapter 4) because they
provide a transition to Alexander Nehamas's radically different
approach to Socratic irony.

Alexander Nehamas: Socratic Irony as Silence

Nehamas shares the conviction – with Lear and Rorty – that irony
reveals something philosophically important about living a human
life. He seeks to recover the role of irony in philosophy as the "art of
living" – a tradition that began with Socrates. He begins his book,
The Art of Living, by distinguishing two traditions in philosophy: philosophy as a theoretical discipline and philosophy as the art of living.
The former is the dominant tradition in contemporary philosophy
(although it has its roots in ancient philosophy). From a theoretical
perspective, we want to know what there is, what is true, and what is
right and good. The aim of theoretical philosophy is to get things
right and "what philosophers study makes no more claim to affecting
their personal lives than the work of physicists, mathematics, or
economics is expected to affect theirs" (Nehamas 1998: 1). When

philosophy is practiced as an academic discipline – as it is throughout the world today – it is theoretical in this broad sense. But there is another tradition that also has its origins in classical Greece: *philosophy as a way of life*, or, to use Nehamas's suggestive phrase, "the art of living" (τέχνη τοῦ βίου).

> We are therefore faced with at least two conceptions of philosophy. One avoids personal style and idiosyncrasy as much as possible. Its aim is to deface the particular personality that offers answers to philosophical questions, since all that matters is the quality of the answers and not the nature of the character who offers them. The other requires style and idiosyncrasy, because its readers must never forget that the views that confront them are the views of a particular type of person and no one else. (Nehamas 1998: 3)[14]

Each type of philosophy has been (and continues to be) suspicious of the other.[15] Both traditions can claim to be legitimate developments of philosophy that have their origins in classical Greece. And, like many rough distinctions, this distinction between philosophy as a theoretical discipline and philosophy as the art of living is not fixed and rigid; it is a heuristic device for clarifying different philosophical approaches and emphases.

There is, however, an apparent paradox that stands at the heart of Nehamas's book. He wants to show how three modern thinkers – Montaigne, Nietzsche, and Foucault – create themselves through their *writings*. They are "both the characters their writings generate and the authors of the writings in which their characters exist. They are creators and creatures in one" (Nehamas 1998: 3). They stand in the tradition of the art of living initiated by Socrates. *But Socrates never wrote anything*! So the art of living expressed in writing is based on a figure who never wrote anything. The Socrates that Nehamas takes to initiate the art of living tradition is himself a literary character created by Plato – not the living historical Socrates that Vlastos thinks he has discovered in the early Platonic dialogues. "But had not Plato created an art of living in [Socrates'] name – and in writing – there would be nothing for us to think about, no art and no model to accept, reject, manipulate, or even to pass by indifferently" (Nehamas 1998: 8). If we are to pursue the variations on the art of living in such thinkers as Montaigne, Nietzsche, and Foucault, then we need to go back to the source and understand what is distinctive about Socratic irony.[16] The Socrates of the early Platonic dialogues "is a mystery because of his irony, his persistent silence about himself, which has given rise to a swirl of voices surrounding it and trying to speak for him, to explain who he was and how he came to be that way. But no interpretation, no other voice, has filled the silence that remains Socrates' main legacy" (Nehamas 1998: 9). If we view Socrates as a *character* created by Plato, then there is a preliminary issue that we need to confront – *Plato's irony*.[17] Nehamas sharply distinguishes Plato's irony (that of the author of the dialogues) from the irony of the main character that Plato has created – Socrates. He stresses two features of Platonic irony. Plato beguiles us into identifying ourselves with Socrates. "Since Socrates' attitude towards his interlocutors is ironic, so is ours" (Nehamas 1998: 12). At the same time, Plato shows us that we have no grounds for thinking that we are superior to Socrates' "victims."

Plato's Socrates is an ambiguous figure, who seems to be at once ordinary – a part of this earthly world – and yet totally strange and extraordinary. Nehamas singles out two distinctive features of Platonic irony: "Both features – inducing self-deception in one's readers as one is depicting it in one's characters and constructing a hero whom it is impossible to understand once and for all – constitute a deeply ironical relationship between author and audience" (Nehamas 1998: 11). This is the heart of Plato's irony – a triadic ironic relation that involves (a) Plato the author; (b) the characters he has created – Socrates and his discussants; and (c) the *audience* – the readers of the dialogues. Plato's irony is directed toward the *readers* of his dialogues because he beguiles them into identifying their point of view with that of Socrates. We feel superior to characters like Euthyphro. Nevertheless, this reaction is our undoing because, although ironists always make an implicit claim to be superior to their victims, Plato shows us that we – the readers of the dialogues – have *no* grounds for claiming this.

We can better grasp what Nehamas means by Platonic irony by turning to the way in which he analyzes Plato's *Euthyphro*. Many interpreters of the *Euthyphro* have commented on the obtuseness and stupidity of Euthyphro. Why did Plato create such a character? "Why then is Euthyphro so stupid, and why is Socrates' irony toward him so heavy handed?" (Nehamas 1998: 39). Euthyphro lacks any glimmer of self-knowledge. He is confused and self-deceived, but we readers presumably know better and see through Euthyphro's self-deception.

So what do we do? We finish reading the dialogue and go about our usual business, just as Euthyphro remembers that he has an appointment and hurries off without ever answering Socrates' questions.

> We too go about our usual business, just as [Euthyphro] proposes to do. And our usual business does not normally center on becoming conscious of and fighting against the self-delusion that characterizes Euthyphro and that, as we turn away from the dialogue, we demonstrate to be ruling our own lives as well – *which is really the aim of this whole mechanism.* Socrates' irony is directed at Euthyphro only as a means; its real goal are the readers of Plato's dialogue. (Nehamas 1998: 41, Nehamas' emphasis)

In short, Plato's portrayal of the encounter between Socrates and Euthyphro is not primarily intended to expose the obtuseness of Euthyphro. *Platonic irony is directed at us – the readers of the dialogue.* Only if we become aware of our own self-deception and ignorance do we experience the full *sting* of Plato's irony.

Summing up his reading of the Socratic dialogues as exercises in Platonic irony, Nehamas declares: "The Socratic dialogues demand of their audience what Socrates asks of his interlocutors: to examine their beliefs on any subject of importance to them, to determine to what other beliefs they are logically related, to accept only those that are compatible with one another, and to live their lives accordingly. That is a question we are as good at ignoring as any of Socrates' simple interlocutors" (Nehamas 1998: 42).

Lear's discussion of "ironic uptake" is helpful for understanding Nehamas's point. If we are beguiled, if we simply identify with Socrates (even if we criticize Socrates), if we limit ourselves to a careful analysis of the arguments, characters, and dramatic settings of the dialogues, there isn't any ironic uptake. We are engaging in left-hand reflection as good students of Platonic texts. But if we begin to realize that Plato's irony is directed at *us* – the readers – that we may not have better answers to Socrates' questions than the interlocutors in the dialogues, that we need to question ourselves about the type of questions Socrates is raising about piety, justice, temperance, courage, and wisdom, then we *may* experience ironic uptake and engage in right-hand questioning. We, the readers, may begin to experience uncanny ironic disruption and actively engage in the examined life.[18]

Plato lures the readers of his early dialogues into a cunningly induced state of confident ignorance. He instills confidence by lulling us into believing that we know better than Socrates' interlocutors. He makes us presume that, unlike them, we see Socrates' point; he makes us imagine that we agree, if not with every single one of Socrates' views, at least with his general outlook on life. And he displays our ignorance by showing that in fact we do nothing of the sort. He forces us to see that although we agree with Socrates' uncompromising demand to devote our life to the pursuit of reason and virtue, we remain ultimately indifferent to it. (Nehamas 1998: 46)

If Socratic irony is a necessary element of Platonic irony, what precisely does Nehamas think Socratic irony is? Earlier I cited Vlastos's claim that irony is a figure of speech or trope "in which something contrary to what is said is to be understood." Vlastos sharply distinguishes irony (which he claims doesn't involve deception) from the Greek *eirōneia* whose *primary* meaning is to willfully deceive. Nehamas begins his discussion of Socratic irony by criticizing Vlastos's thesis. Vlastos's analysis of Socratic irony is based upon a sharp binary opposition between truthfulness and lying, but this simple contrast "cannot capture either Socrates' character or his way of doing philosophy" (Nehamas 1998: 59). What Nehamas finds most objectionable in Vlastos's account of Socratic irony is that irony becomes *transparent*.[19] If irony were simply expressing what we mean by saying something contrary to what we say, then we should easily be able to discern what the ironist really means. It is simply the *opposite* of what Socrates actually says. But this is what Nehamas contests.[20] Socratic irony involves *concealment*. "Intermediate between lying and truthfulness, it shares features with both: like truthfulness, concealment does not distort the truth; like lying, it does not reveal it. Once we have rejected the view that irony consists simply in saying the contrary of what you mean, concealment cannot, even when the irony is detected, lead us to the ironist's real meaning" (Nehamas 1998: 62).[21]

To illustrate what he means by concealment, Nehamas returns to Alcibiades' speech in the *Symposium* that Vlastos also discusses in his analysis of Socratic irony. Vlastos concedes that Alcibiades was deceived, but claims that he was not deceived by Socrates, but rather by himself. "He believed what he did [that Socrates wanted to have sex with him] because he wanted to believe it" (Vlastos 1991: 41). Nehamas sharply disagrees with Vlastos's reading.

Even though Socrates may never have intended to deceive Alcibiades, his toying with him, his concealing himself and his real desire behind his words, prompted the boy into the wrong reaction. Perhaps Alcibiades did want to believe that Socrates wanted him, but it was Socrates himself, through his irony, who helped him transform his belief into action. Vlastos tries to absolve Socrates of all responsibility for Alcibiades' reaction. I believe he tempted him into it, if only to teach him a further lesson. (Nehamas 1998: 62)[22]

Nehamas sums up his understanding of Socratic irony (and how it differs from Vlastos's interpretation) when he writes:

If we take irony as saying the contrary of what you mean, then the meaning of an ironic statement is perfectly clear. If we take it, more generally, as saying something other than what you mean, the meaning of an ironic statement is much less determinate. It can remain hidden even from those who know full well that you are being ironic. And it always suggests that you are holding back something you do not consider your audience worthy of knowing. It constitutes a refusal to put yourself on the same level as your audience. And even though it may intimate that you may be uncertain about your own intention, it still presents you as superior: for that is an uncertainty you do not openly reveal. (Nehamas 1998: 63)[23]

Even if we accept Nehamas's critique of Vlastos and his claim that Socratic irony involves a type of concealment that doesn't fall neatly into the binary opposition of truthfulness or deceit, we still want to know how it is related to the art of living.[24] The key lies in understanding what Nehamas means by Socrates' *silence*. He cites a passage from Kierkegaard's *The Concept of Irony*, which he uses as an epigraph in his chapter, "Socratic Irony: Character and Author": "Socrates' life is like a magnificent pause in the course of history: we do not hear him at all; a profound stillness prevails – until it is broken by the noisy attempts of the many and different schools of followers to trace their origin in this hidden and cryptic source. His irony was not the instrument he used in the service of the idea; irony was his position – more he did not have" (cited in Nehamas 1998: 70).[25]

Commenting on this passage, Nehamas writes: "The idea that the most voluble figure in the history of philosophy is someone 'we do not hear at all' seems at first to be just a calculated effort to shock and unsettle. But Kierkegaard is serious" (Nehamas 1998: 70).[26] And Nehamas is serious too! What does he mean by Socrates' silence? Of course he is not denying the obvious – that Socrates, the character created by Plato in his early dialogues, is always engaged in conversation and in elenctic encounters with his interlocutors. Despite everything that Socrates says, and everything that has been said in his name throughout the ages, right up to the present, Socrates still remains a strange (*atopos*) mysterious figure – at once worldly and unworldly. We never really know quite what he knows and believes.[27] Plato's genius is to have created a character who continually fascinates and provokes us to interpret and reinterpret not only what he means in his ironic remarks, but also how he managed to live such a distinctive life.[28] Nehamas even claims that Plato created a character that even he doesn't completely understand. "Socrates is a paradox not only for the dialogues' readers but, more important and more paradoxical for his own student, his own author. That paradox animates those works and their hero and makes it necessary to return to them again and again in the search of the 'real' Socrates" (Nehamas 1998: 86). Plato compels us to ask all sorts of questions about Socrates that we can't answer in any definitive manner.[29] How did Socrates become Socrates? How did he create himself?[30] What does he really believe, and what does he know? How does he manage to live such an exemplary virtuous life – exhibiting the virtues of courage, self-control, justice, and wisdom – when he claims to be ignorant? Why was he attracted to characters like Alcibiades and others who turned out to be vicious? When Socrates agrees to spend the night with Alcibiades, wasn't he really leading him on? Socrates could not have been so naïve as not to grasp what Alcibiades really wanted.

When Nehamas speaks of Socrates' silence, he is suggesting that there are no *definitive* answers to the many questions that we raise about Socrates' motives, intentions, desires, and beliefs – and yet we feel compelled to answer these questions on Socrates' behalf. And what is so fascinating and admirable about this character is that he appears to live a life that many of us (although not all) want to emulate.[31] He stands as an exemplar of what it is to live a philosophical life – to be a genuine lover of wisdom. Yet, when we ask what it really means to follow Socrates' example, once again we encounter only *our* interpretations of what is distinctive about his art of living; we are met with Socrates' silence. How, then, does Nehamas understand Socratic irony – the ironist that the ironic Plato created in the character of Socrates?

We have seen that irony does not always, and never in the most interesting cases, mean the contrary of what it says. More often, ironists distance themselves, in a variety of ways, from the words they use. They are unwilling to accept full responsibility for what they say, but they are equally unwilling to deny it explicitly: as Kierkegaard put it, they remain "negatively free." Irony presents what seems at first sight a mask. Sometimes it presents a real mask. Sometimes it leaves the question open whether we really see a mask or, if we do, what, if anything, it is a mask of. Irony creates an essential uncertainty. It makes it impossible to decide whether ironists are or are not serious, either about that they say or about what they mean. Sometimes it makes it impossible to know whether ironists even know who they really are... That is Socrates' final and most complex irony. He disavows the knowledge he himself considers necessary for a life of *aretè*. But he is also "serenely" confident in thinking he has actually lived such a life. And we have no reason to believe that he himself had a view about how that, how *he*, was possible. But since he did live a good life, does he or does he not think he really has that knowledge? Does he or does he not mean his disavowal seriously? (Nehamas 1998: 86–7).[32]

We, the readers of the Platonic dialogues, are also confident that Socrates has lived a life of *aretè* – although we remain perplexed about how living such a life is compatible with his professions of ignorance.[33]

Vlastos and Nehamas: Productive Tensions

At first glance it would seem that Vlastos's and Nehamas's understandings of Socratic irony are radically opposed. But although I do not think that their differences can be reconciled, they are not nearly as different as they may initially appear.[34] Nehamas has a tendency to overstate his differences with his former teacher, but there is actually a productive tension between them.

Let us consider again the way in which Vlastos characterizes complex irony. "In 'complex' irony what is said both is and isn't what is meant: its content is meant to be true in one sense, false in another" (Vlastos 1991: 31). In referring to the great philosophical paradoxes in Plato's dialogues, such as Socrates' disavowal of knowledge and teaching, Vlastos thinks that each of the different meanings of these key concepts becomes intelligible only as complex irony.

Notice that, in this context, Vlastos does not speak of "contraries." He does not imply – as Nehamas claims he does – that complex irony is completely transparent. If we are dealing with the disavowal of knowledge, then the difficult task is to figure out the *sense* in which Socrates is ignorant and the *sense* in which he has some sort of knowledge. This is also true when figuring out in what sense Socrates *is* and *is not* a teacher. I don't see that Nehamas really disagrees with this. Nehamas emphasizes the importance of the question: "How can we understand Socrates' disavowal of knowledge when we are confronted with his claims to know that these things are true?" (Nehamas 1998: 73). I think that the disagreement between Vlastos and Nehamas is *not* about what Vlastos characterizes as complex irony, but rather about how we are to *resolve* the conflict of meanings by an appeal to different senses of knowing and teaching – that is, how to resolve the apparent paradox that Socrates is ignorant and yet claims to know that he has led a just life. I also think that Vlastos is right (and I am not sure that Nehamas would disagree) that, throughout the Platonic dialogues, we do find many instances of "complex irony" – where the task is to figure out in what sense the ironic claim is true and in what sense it is false. But even conceding this, we should not neglect Nehamas's point that, all too frequently, Socrates' meaning is *indeterminate*. Or, to use an expression of Derrida's, the precise meaning of Socratic irony is *undecidable*. Consequently we, the readers, *cannot* always say in what sense Socrates' meaning is true and in what sense it is false. I also think that Nehamas is right when he argues that Vlastos's rigid dichotomy between willful deception and innocence – which underlies his entire analysis of irony – fails to do justice to the intractable ambiguity of Socratic irony. Vlastos's binary opposition also reinforces an idealized image of Socrates – as someone who is beyond playing tricks on his interlocutors or even willfully tying them up in aporias. Despite Socrates' manifest criticism of the Sophists, Socrates is a master of sophistic rhetorical devices.

The primary difference between Vlastos and Nehamas concerns the relation of Socratic irony to the art of living. Earlier I mentioned a problem in Vlastos's analysis. Vlastos's major claim is that "Socrates changes the primary meaning of *eirōneia* from deceit to irony not by theorizing about it but by creating something new for it to mean, a new form of life realized in himself." We can read Nehamas as trying to elucidate what Vlastos mentions so casually but does not adequately explain. The key to Socratic irony is not simply what

Socrates *says*, but what he *does*, how he lives his life – especially as he is portrayed by Plato. And what he *does* manifest is the creation of a new form of life that exemplifies irony. This is why Socratic irony is so philosophically important. "Ironically," Vlastos comes close to making a similar point about the significance of what Socrates *does* when he tells us that one of Socrates' chief claims to fame is "his contribution to the sensibility of Western Europe, no less memorable an achievement than is his contribution to our moral philosophy" (Vlastos 1991: 43). Nehamas helps us to make sense of this claim, and consequently he avoids the trivialization of irony when it is taken to be *exclusively* "the use of words to express something other than, and especially the opposite of, [their] literal meaning."[35]

How does our discussion of these conflicting interpretations of Socratic irony relate to the characterization of irony by Lear and Rorty? Both Lear and Rorty would certainly endorse Nehamas's claim that irony is a form of life, as suggested by Vlastos, but really only developed by Nehamas in his depiction of the art of living. Lear's reflections on ironic uptake are, as I have indicated, helpful for grasping what Nehamas claims is characteristic of irony. If we restrict ourselves to analyzing irony as a figure of speech or a trope, we are likely to miss the philosophical import of irony. We are likely to limit ourselves to what Lear labels left-hand reflection – and never make the transition to right-hand questioning. We *can* read the Platonic dialogues as setting a task exclusively for left-hand reflection. But if we read the dialogues as speaking to *us* – the readers of the dialogues – if we try ourselves to confront the aporias of Socrates' irony; if we seriously try to grapple with such questions as what is piety, what is justice, what is courage, and what is wisdom; then the power of Platonic and Socratic irony may be realized in our *own* art of living. Lear is right when he indicates that this occurs *only* where there is ironic uptake – that is, when we are genuinely disoriented, when there is a breakdown in normal left-hand reflection. Rorty certainly would welcome Nehamas's reading of the enigmatic Socrates – the Socrates that we never seem to really pin down. He would welcome Nehamas's characterization of three genres or varieties of the art of living: the first exemplified by the Socrates of Plato's early dialogues in which Socrates cannot show that his mode of life is right for all; the second represented by Plato's middle dialogues in which Plato, inspired by the life of Socrates, argues that the life of philosophy is best for all; and the third, the "aestheticist" art of living, whereby individuals seek

poetically to create themselves. Rorty, like Nehamas, is most interested in this third genre in which one is engaged in the activity of
aesthetic self-creation. He is critical of the second sense of the art of
living because, like Nietzsche, Rorty thinks that it leads to a false
sense of universal rationality. Concerning the Socrates of the early
dialogues, Rorty would say that we should take Socrates' profession
of ignorance seriously. So when Socrates asks such questions as what
is piety, what is courage, or what is justice, we should not think that
there are (or ought to be) universal answers to these questions.
Rather, the point of Socratic irony is that *neither* Socrates *nor* any of
his interlocutors can satisfactorily answer such questions. Rorty does
think that, even if the Socratic virtues cannot be defended by Platonic
means, they can be *practiced* "without any metaphysical comfort"
(Rorty 1982: 174).

Earlier I quoted Lear's claim that Socrates' ironic questioning
seems to maintain a "weird balancing act: simultaneously (i) calling
into question a practical identity (as socially understood), (ii) living
that identity, (iii) declaring ignorance of what it consists in" (Lear
2011: 24). We can interpret these remarks in a way that is compatible
with both Rorty's and Nehamas's claims about Socratic irony. Rorty
would agree that Socrates calls into question the conventional understanding of living a virtuous life. This is what most of the early
Platonic dialogues are about. And yes, Socrates does live an eminently virtuous life – at least, this is what Plato invites us to believe.
Finally, we have to take him at his word when he declares that he is
ignorant of what living such a virtuous life consists in. Lear's claims
are also compatible with what Nehamas calls Socrates' silence –
where this means that we are invited, indeed required, to interpret
and to *answer for* Socrates when he remains silent. In the early dialogues, neither Socrates nor any of his interlocutors come up with
satisfactory answers to the questions he raises. So we have good
reason to take his ignorance seriously. Socrates is always questioning
conventional practical identities – in particular, the practical identity
of living a virtuous life. Nevertheless, although Socrates fails to
develop a satisfactory *theoretical* account of virtue (in the early dialogues), Plato portrays Socrates as *living* a virtuous life – *practicing*
virtue even in the face of death.

Lear, Rorty, and Nehamas are primarily concerned with retrieving
a tradition in philosophy that is in danger of being lost and forgotten
– effaced by a theoretical approach that loses sight of the art of

living. And even Vlastos, who might be described as a paradigmatic theoretical philosopher, indicates his appreciation of Socrates as creating a new personality and form of life. All four view irony as much more than a clever figure of speech. They are *not* engaging in nostalgia or advocating a return to the Greeks, but they are showing that we can learn something vital about how to live a human life from Plato's portrayal of Socratic irony. Although speaking of Socrates' silence is perhaps a hyperbolic way of describing Socrates, Nehamas is insightful in suggesting that Plato's genius is to have created a character who is at once mysterious, ambiguous, and thoroughly strange (*atopos*). Socrates is someone about whom no one has the last word or the final interpretation. Plato's Socrates provokes ever new nuances of interpretation (and critique). Despite my criticisms of Lear, Rorty, Vlastos, and Nehamas, I believe that each contributes something *vital* to a philosophical understanding of irony that shapes the art of living. All four might well agree with Karl Jaspers when he writes: "[S]ome image of Socrates is indispensable to our philosophic thinking. Perhaps we may say that today no philosophic thought is possible unless Socrates is present, if only as a pale shadow. The way in which a man experiences Socrates is fundamental to his thinking" (Jaspers 1962: 20).

Chapter 3

Søren Kierkegaard: Irony and Ethical Passion

There is a specter haunting our discussion of irony – and it is the specter of Kierkegaard. Lear, Rorty, Vlastos, and Nehamas all refer to Kierkegaard at central points in their discussions of irony. Before turning to the texts of Kierkegaard, I want to review what each of them has to say about Kierkegaard. Like the proverbial story of the blind man touching different parts of the elephant, each appeals to (or criticizes) a different aspect of Kierkegaard.

Kierkegaard is most prominent in Lear's case for irony. I have mentioned Lear's striking claim that Kierkegaard has everywhere been his teacher about irony. Insofar as we want to grasp what irony "really is," we need to grasp "what should matter when it comes to living a distinctively human life" (Lear 2011: p. ix). Lear thinks that both Vlastos and Nehamas are mistaken about Kierkegaard, because they mistakenly regard *The Concept of Irony* as providing Kierkegaard's settled view of irony. They miss what "from a Kierkegaardian perspective, makes irony such a philosophically and ethically powerful phenomenon" (Lear 2011: 184, n. 38). Lear thinks that his positive claims about irony are a proper explication of what Kierkegaard means by irony.

Rorty does not explicitly mention Kierkegaard when he gives his definition of irony and the "liberal ironist" in *Contingency, Irony, and Solidarity*, but references to Kierkegaard appear throughout Rorty's writings. In *Contingency, Irony, and Solidarity*, he cites Kierkegaard's remark about Hegel's *Science of Logic*. Kierkegaard tells us that "if

Hegel had prefaced his work with 'This is all just a thought-experiment,' he would have been the greatest thinker who ever lived" (Rorty 1989: 104). Rorty's insouciant remarks on the relation between Hegel and Kierkegaard are relevant to his own conception of irony.

> It would be charitable and pleasant, albeit unjustified by the evidence, to believe that Hegel deliberately refrained from speculating on the nation which would succeed Germany, and the philosopher who would succeed Hegel, because he wanted to demonstrate his own awareness of his own finitude through what Kierkegaard called "indirect communication" by an ironic gesture rather than by putting forward a claim. It would be nice to think that he deliberately left the future blank as an invitation to his successors to do to him what he had done to his predecessors, rather than as an arrogant assumption that nothing more could possibly be done. But, however it may have been with Hegel, the problem of how to finitize while exhibiting a knowledge of one's own finitude – of satisfying Kierkegaard's demand on Hegel – is *the* problem of ironist theory. (Rorty 1989: 104–5)

Kierkegaard, for Rorty, is this edifying (*opbyggelige*) thinker who is reactive to his times and offers "satires, parodies, aphorisms."

Vlastos's remarks about Kierkegaard are sparse. He believes, however, that Kierkegaard goes wrong when he claims that deceit is a component of Socratic irony. According to Vlastos, Socrates doesn't even use deceit as a debating tactic. "Some of Socrates' most devoted students have taken it for granted that he does. For Kierkegaard, Socrates is the anti-sophist who by ironies of sophistry tricks sophists into truth" (Vlastos 1991: 42).[1] To explain Socratic irony, Vlastos has "gone back to the primary, down-to-earth, meaning of the living word which 'irony' has been in all the languages of the Western world, beginning with Cicero's Latin. In this primary form which all philosophically invented ones (including the one Kierkegaard fished out of Hegel: 'infinite absolute negativity') what irony means is simply expressing what we mean by saying something contrary to it" (Vlastos 1991: 43). Kierkegaard's "treatment of irony is hopelessly perplexed by this dazzling mystification. It seduces him into finding in the Platonic texts he purports to be glossing the vagaries of a romantic novella: 'the disguise and mysteriousness which it [irony] entails... the infinite sympathy it assumes, the elusive and ineffable moment of understanding immediately displaced by the anxiety of misunderstanding' etc." (Vlastos 1991: 43, n. 81). But although Vlastos claims that Kierkegaard misunderstands Socratic irony, he acknowledges "that in the persona of Socrates depicted by Plato there is something which helps to explain what Kierkegaard's genius... [has] read into Socrates" (Vlastos 1991: 44).

Although Nehamas, like Vlastos, is primarily concerned with understanding Socratic irony, Kierkegaard plays a significant role in his analysis. Kierkegaard inspires his thesis about Socrates' *silence*. Recall the passage quoted earlier from *The Concept of Irony*: "Socrates' life is like a magnificent pause in the course of history: we do not hear him at all: a profound silence prevails" (Nehamas 1998: 70). Nehamas also appeals to Kierkegaard in order to develop Quintilian's notion that Socrates' *whole life* was characterized by irony. But Nehamas (like Kierkegaard) does not accept "Quintilian's further view that Socrates' irony is nothing but feigned ignorance. This most common understanding of Socratic irony must be rejected. Socrates does not feign the ignorance we find him avowing in Plato's early works" (Nehamas 1998: 72).[2] Nevertheless, Nehamas is not an uncritical admirer of Kierkegaard's view of Socrates and Socratic irony. Nehamas believes that, despite his admiration for Socrates, Kierkegaard claims that Socrates was a Sophist who used sophistry against the Sophists. But although Socrates was part of the sophist movement, Nehamas says that "our image of Socrates makes it impossible to attribute to him outright, intentional deceptiveness" (Nehamas 1998: 57). (Nehamas, as we have seen, rejects the rigid alternatives of *either* honesty *or* fraud. The dilemma posed by the question "Is Socrates sincerely honest or is he a willful deceiver?" is misleading. We need a more nuanced description of Socratic irony.)

What is striking about Lear and Nehamas is that despite their disagreements, they *both* take Kierkegaard as their guide for developing their interpretations of Socratic irony. Vlastos acknowledges Kierkegaard's "genius," but accuses him of misunderstanding Socratic irony. Yet this accusation sticks only if we accept Vlastos's understanding of "complex irony" as the key to understanding Socratic irony. I am in sympathy with Nehamas's and Lear's critiques of Vlastos. Complex irony, as Vlastos understands it, is far too simple a concept to grasp Socratic irony. It is not sufficient to help explain how Socrates created a new form of life. (This is not to deny that *some* of Socrates' uses of irony exemplify the structure of complex irony.) Rorty is deeply sympathetic with the Kierkegaardian theme that irony is not simply a figure of speech, but a way of living a human life.

Now let us turn to Kierkegaard himself: how he understands Socratic irony, why irony is so central to his thinking. This task is far more difficult than one might at first imagine – and Kierkegaard sets all sorts of traps and obstacles in our way. Let us review some of the obstacles that confront any interpreter of Kierkegaard. The first serious problem is that there are very different types of sources that one needs to take into account. Then there are the writings that Kierkegaard published in his own name. Then there are the pseudonymous works (and there are many different pseudonymous authors). Sometimes these pseudonymous characters discuss other pseudonymous characters. And finally, there are Kierkegaard's extensive journals and papers. Irony is discussed in all these works. This, however, is only the beginning of our problems. *The Concept of Irony with Continual Reference to Socrates* was Kierkegaard's Magister dissertation published in 1841 when he was 28 years old. It was published before any of his major pseudonymous works. Some of his pseudonymous authors, especially Johannes Climacus, have a great deal to say about irony and humor. And Climacus even makes fun of some of the things that are written in *The Concept of Irony*. Indeed, there is a long section of *Concluding Unscientific Postscript* in which Johannes Climacus critically comments on the previous books published by other pseudonymous creations of Kierkegaard. So we have the complex situation of Climacus (a character created by Kierkegaard) assuming the position of a reader of, and commentator on, the previous pseudonymous authors (created by Kierkegaard), who themselves disown responsibility for what they have written. Kierkegaard warns us over and over again not to confuse what is said in these books with *his* views.[3] At the end of *Concluding Unscientific Postscript*, Kierkegaard (in his own name) signs "A First and Last Declaration." He acknowledges that he is the legal author of his pseudonymous books, but declares:

> What has been written [in the pseudonymous works], then, is mine, but only insofar as I, by means of audible lines, have placed the life-view of the crea*ting*, poetically actual individuality in his mouth, for my relation is even more remote than that of a poet, who *poetizes* characters and yet in the preface is *himself* the *author*. That is, I am impersonally or personally in the third person a *souffleur* [prompter] who has poetically produced the *authors*, whose *prefaces* in turn are their productions, as their *names* are also. Thus in the pseudonymous books there is not a single word by me. (Kierkegaard 1992: 625–6)

And Kierkegaard adds: "Therefore, if it should occur to anyone to want to quote a particular passage from the books, it is my wish, my prayer, that he will do me the kindness of citing the respective pseudonymous author's name, not mine" (Kierkegaard 1992: 627). So one may begin to have the unsettling experience in reading Kierkegaard and his pseudonymous authors that one is in a hall of mirrors, where one can never quite figure out who (if anyone) is the "real" Kierkegaard and who is only a pale or vivid reflection. Or, to switch metaphors, the experience of reading Kierkegaard can be like being in an echo chamber, where it is impossible to discern where the voice that echoes through the chamber is coming from. I will argue that the ultimate thrust of the writings of Kierkegaard and his pseudonymous authors is directed to *us* the readers – to dispel *our* illusions and compel us to face up to our confusions and our ignorance. For this is the only way that we can confront ourselves (make the commitments, decisions, and choices) that are required for each of us as "single individuals" to *become* existing human beings – in short, to change our lives. This is why Kierkegaard fits so well in the tradition of the art of living. For Kierkegaard, irony is essential for living a genuinely *human* life. There is an analogy here with the way in which Nehamas describes Platonic irony. Recall that Nehamas argued that, in his early dialogues, Plato seduces us into thinking that we can identify with the ironic stance that Socrates takes toward his interlocutors. Thus we can feel a sense of superiority that we are not as dumb or obtuse as some of Socrates' interlocutors. But the real sting of Platonic irony is to make *us* – the readers – feel uncomfortable and disoriented when it dawns on us that we don't really have any better answers to Socrates' questions than the "Euthyphros" of this world. So, too, when we seek to understand what Climacus is telling us about truth in the *Postscript*, we may think (delude ourselves) that we "get it" when we proclaim that "Truth is Subjectivity." We may even become town criers of the new truth "Truth is Subjectivity." This, however, becomes a way of *avoiding* and defending ourselves against the need to face up to our confusions, to face up to what it means for each of us "to become an existing human being."[4]

With these preliminary warnings, I want to consider some of the highlights of what Kierkegaard and his pseudonymous authors say about irony.[5] I plan to focus on the discussion of Socratic irony in *The Concept of Irony* and in *Concluding Unscientific Postscript*.

Irony as Infinite Absolute Negativity

In 1841, when Kierkegaard submitted his Magister dissertation, candidates were expected to write in Latin. Kierkegaard had to petition the King for special permission to write in Danish, although his public defense (which lasted seven and a half hours) was conducted in Latin. He attached fifteen short theses in Latin at the beginning of the dissertation. I mention this because the fifteenth (final) thesis is so revealing: *Ut a dubitatione philosophia sic ab ironia vita digna, quae humana vocetur, incipit* ("Just as philosophy begins with doubt, so also a life that may be called human begins with irony"). The Latin phrase "vita digna" can also be translated as "a life *worthy* of being called human begins with irony" (Kierkegaard 1989: 5–6).[6]

Like many dissertations, *The Concept of Irony* is extremely ponderous and wordy – although we will see that, at crucial moments, the passionate and witty Kierkegaard bursts forth. In light of Kierkegaard's later radical turn against Hegel, it is striking that his dissertation is filled with the Hegelian jargon that was so fashionable at the time in Danish philosophical circles. The very title of the book reveals the Hegelian imprint. In Danish, the title is *Om Begrebet Ironi. Begreb* is the Danish translation of the German *Begriff*, perhaps the most important expression in the Hegelian lexicon. And it is intriguing – in light of Kierkegaard's (and his pseudonyms') subsequent relentless attacks on Hegel, Hegelians, and "speculative philosophy" – that he juxtaposes (*Begreb*) *Concept* and (*Ironi*) *Irony*. Concept and irony turn out to be thoroughly incompatible with each other.[7] Indeed – to judge by the criterion advanced by Johannes Climacus in the *Concluding Unscientific Postscript* – the juxtaposition of concept and irony is incongruous and comical.

Hegel and Hegelianism not only heavily influenced the language of *The Concept of Irony*, but also appear to shape the structure of the book. It consists of two parts. Part One is entitled "The Position of Socrates Viewed as Irony," and in good Hegelian fashion is divided into three sections following the modalities of Possibility, Actuality, and Necessity: "The View Made Possible," "The Actualization of the View," and "The View Made Necessary." Part Two is simply entitled "The Concept of Irony."[8]

In his Introduction, Kierkegaard makes an allusion to the passage in the *Symposium* in which Alcibiades describes how Socrates stood still for the entire night at Potidaea – the *very same passage* that is central for Nehamas's (and Lear's) interpretation of Socratic irony. "[W]hat Socrates himself prized so highly, namely standing still and contemplating – in other words, silence – this is his whole life in terms of world history. He has left nothing by which a later age can judge him, indeed even if I were to imagine myself his contemporary, he would still always be difficult to comprehend" (Kierkegaard 1989: 11–12). It is striking that, at the very beginning of *The Concept of Irony*, Kierkegaard's pithy remarks encapsulate the theses that are central to Lear's and Nehamas's understandings of irony. The fifteenth Latin thesis epitomizes Lear's thesis that "a life that may be called human begins with irony." And the statement in the Introduction to *The Concept of Irony* about Socrates' silence epitomizes Nehamas's thesis about Socratic irony.

Like a good Magister, Kierkegaard begins his dissertation with a discussion of the Socratic problem, reviewing the views of Socrates by Xenophon, Plato, and Aristophanes. Kierkegaard is dismissive of Xenophon because, although Xenophon wanted to show that the condemnation to death of Socrates by the Athenians was a scandalous injustice, he has no sense of "Socrates' personality." Xenophon's depiction is pedestrian, and "with respect to irony, there is not one trace of it in Xenophon" (Kierkegaard 1989: 25).[9] He concludes his discussion of Xenophon by declaring: "This completes my view of Socrates as he stands and walks in Xenophon's puppet box, and in conclusion I only ask my readers, insofar as they have been bored, not to place the blame solely upon me" (Kierkegaard 1989: 27). Kierkegaard discusses Xenophon in just ten pages, but the next hundred pages are dedicated to Plato. Kierkegaard affirms his "youthful infatuation with Plato."

> Dear critic, allow me just one sentence, one guileless parenthesis, in order to vent my gratitude, my gratitude for the relief I found in reading Plato. Where is balm to be found if not in the infinite tranquility with which, in the quiet of the night, the idea soundlessly, solemnly, gently, and yet so powerfully unfurls in the rhythm of the dialogue, as if there were nothing else in the world, where every step is deliberated and repeated slowly, solemnly, because the ideas themselves seem to know that there is time and an arena for all of them? (Kierkegaard 1989: 27–8)

And with regard to the Socratic problem – specifically, the relation of Plato's portrayal of Socrates with the historical Socrates – Kierkegaard's description is at once sophisticated and poetic.

> Plato feels himself so inseparably fused with Socrates in the unity of spirit that for him all knowledge is co-knowledge with Socrates. That this need to hear his own professions from the mouth of Socrates after the latter's death must have become even more acute, that for him Socrates had to rise transfigured from his grave to an even more intimately shared life, that the confusion between mine and thine had to increase now, since for Plato, however much he humbled himself, however inferior he felt about adding anything to Socrates' image it was still impossible not to mistake the poetic image for the historical reality – all this is certainly obvious. (Kierkegaard 1989: 30)

What excites Kierkegaard about Plato's portrayal of Socrates (especially in what he takes to be the Socratic dialogues) is that Socrates' *personality* comes alive. And what he means by Socrates' personality is close to what Vlastos calls a "form of life" and Nehamas calls the "the art of living." It is not simply what Socrates *says* that is ironical, but Socrates' personality and the *way he lives his life is his irony*.

But for all Kierkegaard's admiration for the Platonic dialogues, especially those in which Socrates' personality is prominent, he is skeptical of the way in which Plato idealizes Socrates. So, in order to develop a more concrete and realistic image of Socrates, Kierkegaard examines how Aristophanes portrays Socrates. Kierkegaard tells us: "Plato and Aristophanes do have in common an ideality of depiction, but at opposite poles; Plato has the tragic ideality, Aristophanes the comic" (Kierkegaard 1989: 128). Kierkegaard is fully aware of the risks involved in reconstructing Socrates' personality on the basis of the portrayals of Xenophon, Plato, and Aristophanes, but he nevertheless believes that by playing off the different representations of Socrates against each other – by seeing what they emphasize and de-emphasize – we can come close to understanding Socrates' distinctive personality.[10] What, then, is distinctive about Socrates' personality? How is it related to Socrates' silence? In what sense is Socrates the personification of the ironist? How does this enable us to understand the claim that "life that may be called human begins with irony"? In order to answer these questions, I want to take what may initially seem like an indirect approach, but it will take us to the heart of the matter. I want to compare what Hegel says about Socrates and Socratic irony with Kierkegaard. We will see how much Kierkegaard appropriates from Hegel and the precise point where he *swerves* away from Hegel.

The most detailed discussion of Socrates in Hegel is to be found in his *Lectures on the History of Philosophy*. According to Hegel, Socrates makes his appearance on the world historical stage at a crucial transitional stage in Athens when the mythological world view was breaking down. No longer could one rely in a direct, naïve manner on the enigmatic sayings of inspired poets and oracles. If tradition is understood as what is handed down and guides human life, then Hegel sees Athens as undergoing a crisis of tradition. Söderquist succinctly states Hegel's view: "As Hegel sees it, a new consciousness was emerging in which the individual citizen no longer consulted the gods and laws of the state in search of ethical truth but looked rather within the subject, to the desires and thoughts of the individual. This reflective 'moral' [*moralisch*] consciousness, as he calls it, was facilitated in part by a famous group of thinkers: the Sophists" (Söderquist 2013: 60).[11] With the Sophists, there emerges a new reflective consciousness that begins to look within the subject for guidance, rather than to the authority of tradition. "To the Sophists the satisfaction of the individual himself was now made ultimate, and since they made everything uncertain, the fixed point was in the assertion 'it is my desire, my pride, glory, and honour, particular subjectivity, which I made my end'" (Hegel 1968: 370–1). Hegel's characteristic approach to the history of philosophy is illustrated in his treatment of the Sophists. Their original position is based on their destructive attitude toward the existing culture, their questioning of the authority of tradition and the state. And this is achieved by the assertion of the supremacy of individual subjects. This new awareness of reflective subjectivity is a positive achievement for the development of philosophy. But the reason why a movement beyond the Sophists is necessary is because they make everything dependent on the desires and pleasures of *particular* subjects. (Hegel can't resist taking a swipe at his contemporary equivalents of the Greek Sophists: "This takes place also in the present day where the right and true in our actions is made to depend on good intention and on my own conviction" (Hegel 1968: 371).)

Now this is where – according to Hegel's narrative – Socrates enters into "world history." Like the Sophists, Socrates calls into question the authority of tradition. He shares with them the turn to critical reflection by individual subjects. But, unlike the Sophists, Socrates was not satisfied to leave everything to the whim of individual, particular desires. His quarrel with the Sophists is that they have failed to consider the instability and internal conflicting tensions of the desires and pleasures of particular subjects. One needs to *seek the Good* – a universal moral principle. Socratic irony enters the scene in the attempt to reach the Good. Socrates' "ironic questioning" seeks to dissolve existing claims to knowledge, *including* those of the Sophists. In this sense, Socrates' method is even more destructive than that of the Sophists, because he undermines their claims and opinions. But Hegel also underscores the *positive* side of Socrates' questioning. With his maieutic dialectic, Socrates seeks to elicit the recognition of a universal Good. Consequently, Socrates' irony consists in "feigned ignorance."[12] He sought to inspire men with distrust toward their presuppositions.

> Now whether it was that he wished to bring the manner of the Sophists into disrepute, or that he was desirous to awaken the desire for knowledge and independent thought in the youths whom he attracted to himself, he certainly began by adopting the ordinary conceptions which they considered to be true. But in order to bring others to express these, he represents himself as in ignorance of them, and, with a seeming ingenuousness, puts questions to his audience as if they were to instruct him, while he really wished to draw them out. This is the celebrated Socratic irony, which in his case is a particular mode of carrying on intercourse between one person and another, and is thus only a subjective form of dialectic, for real dialectic deals with the reason for things. (Hegel 1968: 398)

Although Socrates advances the story of the actualization of philosophy, he engages only in a "subjective form of dialectic," not "real dialectic." "Thus Socrates taught those with whom he associated to know that they knew nothing; indeed, what is more, he himself said that he knew nothing and therefore taught nothing." And Hegel comments: "It may actually be said that Socrates knew nothing, for he did not reach the systematic construction of a philosophy. He was conscious of this, and it was also not at all his aim to establish a science" (Hegel 1968: 399). The very way in which Hegel describes Socrates, Socratic irony, and Socrates' maieutic method is saturated with Hegel's distinctive terminology and concerns. In describing Socrates' method, he singles out two prominent aspects: "the development of the universal from the concrete case, and the exhibition of the notion [*Begriff*] which implicitly exists in every consciousness" (Hegel 1968: 398). "The irony of Socrates has this great quality of showing how to make abstract ideas concrete and effect their development, for on that alone depends the bringing of the Notion [*Begriff*] into consciousness" (Hegel 1968: 400).

This is where Kierkegaard protests and departs from Hegel. Kierkegaard claims that Hegel's commitment to speculative history and philosophy distorts his understanding of Socrates and Socratic irony. I call this Kierkegaard's *swerve* – his swerve away from Hegel. Kierkegaard accuses Hegel of being impatient with the complexities of Socrates. "[Hegel] uses one single dialogue from Plato as an example of the Socratic method without explaining why he chose this particular one. He uses Xenophon's *Memorabilia* and *Apology*, and also Plato's *Apology*, quite uncritically" (Kierkegaard 1989: 221–2). And in a remark that exhibits Kierkegaard's wit and his use of ironic barb, he writes: "[W]hen the phenomena are paraded, he is in too much of a hurry and is too aware of the great importance of his role as commander-in-chief of world history to take time for more than the royal glance he allows to glide over them...Although he is thereby spared considerable prolixity, he also misses some things that in a complete account would be a necessary element" (Kierkegaard 1989: 222).

What is it that Hegel misses? It is the concrete *personality* of Socrates with all his complexities and contradictions. Initially, however, Kierkegaard's story of what happened in Greek society is very similar to Hegel's. He also stresses that the Sophists and Socrates were reacting to the crisis taking place in Greek society. The authoritative role of ethical and cultural traditions was breaking down. The beautiful world of early Greek society, which was presumably untroubled, no longer existed. With the Sophists, there was – just as Hegel claims – the emergence of a *reflective consciousness* that focuses on the subject. "The immediate consciousness, secure and confident as it relies upon what it receives from the past, like a sacred treasure, scarcely ever notices that life is full of contradictions. Reflection, on the other hand, discovers this at once. It discovers that what is supposed to be absolutely certain, determinative for men (laws, customs, etc.), places the individual in conflict with himself" (Kierkegaard 1989: 204). Thus far Kierkegaard seems to be in complete agreement with Hegel's description of the Sophists. But what was the Sophists' response to this crisis?

> Consequently, it [the Sophists' reflective consciousness] shows the error, but it also has available the remedy for it – it teaches how to give reasons for everything. Thus it gives people an adroitness, a competence in clarifying every particular instance under universal instances; it places at the disposal of each individual a rosary of *loci communes* [general propositions], by repeated recital of which he is in a position of always being able to say something about the particular, make some observations about it, state some reasons for or against. The more such categories one has, the more expert one is in using them, the more educated one is. This was the culture provided by the Sophists. (Kierkegaard 1989: 204)

The Sophists are too quick to think that they have "solved" the problem of the breakdown of tradition. They are too facile in thinking that one can always give *reasons* for or against any particular choice or decision. They fail to appreciate the instability and the internal contradictions of what they advocate.

> But in Sophistry, reflection is awakened; it shakes the foundations of everything, and it is then that Sophistry lulls it to sleep again with reasons. By reasons or *raisonnements*, this hungry monster is satisfied, and thus together with the Sophists the thinker seems able to demonstrate everything, for they could give reasons for everything, and by means of reasons they could at any time whatever make anything whatever true...It appeared, therefore, as if Sophistry were able to constrain the ghost that it itself had raised. But when the foundations of everything have been shaken, what can then become the firm ground that is to save the situation? Either it is the universal (the good, etc.), or it is the finite subject, his propensities, desires, etc. The Sophists seized the latter expedient. (Kierkegaard 1989: 205)

Socrates exposes the instability and internal contradictions of the Sophists. He exposes their false "positivity." He carries out the destructive and negative project of the Sophists in a more thorough and consistent manner.[13] Socrates was "purely negative." "Truth demands silence before it will raise its voice, and Socrates was to bring about this silence" (Kierkegaard 1989: 210). Unlike Hegel (and

Vlastos), Kierkegaard does *not* think that Socrates' ignorance is feigned. Socrates does not *pretend* to be ignorant; he *is* ignorant, and he *knows* that he is ignorant. "[W]hen Socrates declared that he was ignorant, he nevertheless did know something, for he knew about his ignorance; on the other hand, however, this knowledge was not a knowledge of something, that is, did not have a positive content, and to that extent his ignorance was ironic" (Kierkegaard 1989: 269). Kierkegaard recognizes that, in an empirical sense, Socrates was "a very well informed person," but "[i]n a philosophical sense however, he was ignorant. He was ignorant of the ground of all being, the eternal, the divine – that is, he knew that it was, but not what it was" (Kierkegaard 1989: 169). So, unlike Hegel, who already anticipates how world history and the dialectic move on in a more *positive* manner with the appearance of Socrates, Kierkegaard thinks that the "commander-in chief of world history" is projecting his *own* dialectic on to the personality of Socrates. Socratic ignorance is a "true philosophical position and at the same time is also completely negative" (Kierkegaard 1989: 169). We might say, playing on Hegel's own telling phrase, Socrates' irony is "infinite absolute negativity." But even this expression takes on a very different meaning for Kierkegaard. It is *infinite* because it is directed not against this or that particular existing entity, but against the entire given actuality at a certain time. It is thoroughly *negative* because it is incapable of offering any positive alternative. Nothing positive emerges out of this negativity. And it is *absolute* because Socrates refuses to cheat. Unlike the Sophists, Socrates doesn't *pretend* to radically criticize existing actuality and at the same time hold on to some positive position. He is resolute in his negativity.

We can approach Kierkegaard's swerve away from Hegel from another perspective. Hegel frequently draws a sharp distinction between abstract negation and determinate negation. Abstract negation manifests its power as sheer negativity, sheer destructiveness, and results in nothingness or emptiness. But determinate negation is that form of negativity that doesn't result in sheer nothingness, but rather, achieves something *positive* that emerges out of the power of negativity. Determinate negation is the key to understanding the significance of *Aufhebung* – the process of negating, affirming, and passing beyond. One of the most vivid passages in which Hegel describes the power of negativity occurs in the Preface to his *Phenomenology of Spirit*.

But the life of Spirit is not the life that shrinks from death, and keeps itself untouched by devastation, but rather the life that endures it and maintains itself in it. It wins its truth only when in utter dismemberment it finds itself. It is this power, not as something positive, which closes its eyes to the negative, as when we say of something that it is nothing or false, and then having done with it, turn away and pass on to something else; on the contrary, Spirit is this power only by looking the negative in the face and tarrying with it. This tarrying with the negative is the magical power that converts it into being. This power is identical with what we earlier called the Subject, which by giving determinateness an existence in its own element supersedes abstract immediacy, i.e. the immediacy that barely is, and thus is authentic substance: that being or immediacy whose mediation is not outside it but which is this mediation itself. (Hegel 1977: 19, emphasis added)

The precise point where Kierkegaard swerves from Hegel can be located in the above paragraph. Although Hegel is speaking here about Spirit (*Geist*), Kierkegaard would affirm that Socrates' ironic consciousness can be characterized as "looking the negative in the face, and tarrying with it." But this is where Kierkegaard calls a halt. (Kierkegaard would agree with the first three sentences of this passage (the section italicized), but would protest about the rest of it. Hegel, from Kierkegaard's perspective, fails to realize that Socrates never gets beyond "tarrying with the negative."[14] For Kierkegaard, there is no determinate negation here; no mediation emerges from Socrates' negative consciousness.[15] Kierkegaard questions everything that Hegel claims in the non-italicized section of the above passage – at least insofar as it pertains to the personality of Socrates, who is the exemplar of the ironist.[16]

> What Socrates did with the Sophists was to give them the next moment, the moment in which the momentarily true dissolved into nothing – in other words, he let the infinite devour the finite. But Socrates' irony was not turned against only the Sophists, it was turned against the whole established order. He demanded ideality from all of it, and this demand was the judgment that judged and condemned Greek culture. But his irony was not the instrument he used in the service of the idea, irony was his position – more he did not have. If he had the idea, his annihilating activity would not have been so radical. (Kierkegaard 1989: 213–14)[17]

Why is Kierkegaard so insistent on the infinite absolute negativity of Socrates' irony, and why is he so relentless in denying that Socrates has anything positive to offer us? This infinite absolute negativity is the key to understanding Socrates' personality, his *subjectivity*, and *inwardness*. "Just as philosophy begins with doubt, so also a life that may be called human begins with irony." What distinguishes Socrates and makes him the first ironist is the *radicalness* with which he detaches himself and isolates himself from the concrete historical actuality that surrounds him.[18] Socrates refuses to do what the Sophists pretend to do – to act *as if* they are calling everything into question when they are actually smuggling in their particular prejudices, perspectives, and reasons. The failure of the Sophists is the failure to *radicalize* subjectivity and inwardness. By subjectivity, Kierkegaard means the sheer power to ironically negate.[19] In his journals and other writings, Kierkegaard frequently makes critical comments about *The Concept of Irony*.[20] Nevertheless, we discover in *The Concept of Irony* a theme that pervades *all* of Kierkegaard's thinking. It is his insistence on the necessity of an ironic moment – a moment of radical negative freedom that breaks the bonds with all positivity. This is an essential moment in the achievement of personality and in *becoming* a genuine human being.

Thus far, I have been focusing on the first part of *The Concept of Irony*, the first 237 of its 339 pages (in the English translation), that discusses Socrates as the exemplar of the ironist. Part II is entitled "The Concept of Irony." Here Kierkegaard turns to defining the concept of irony. Kierkegaard justifies proceeding in this manner at the very beginning of his dissertation:

> Before I proceed to an exposition of the concept of irony, it is necessary to make sure that I have a reliable and authentic view of Socrates' historical-actual, phenomenological existence with respect to the question of its possible relation to the transformed view that was his fate through enthusiastic or envious contemporaries. This becomes inescapably necessary, because the concept of irony makes its entry into the world with Socrates. Concepts, just like individuals, have their history and are no more able than they to resist the dominion of time, but in and through it all they nevertheless harbor a kind of homesickness for the place of their birth. (Kierkegaard 1989: 9)

After defining the concept of irony in Part II, Kierkegaard turns to a sharp critique of Romantic irony "after Fichte" – especially the Romantic irony of Friedrich Schegel, Ludwig Tieck, and Karl Wilhelm Ferdinand Solger. Here, too, Kierkegaard closely follows Hegel's own damning critique of Romantic irony.[21] Kierkegaard concludes his dissertation with a very brief discussion of the "truth" of irony as a mastered or controlled element. Because the discussion and style of writing in Part II are so different from those in Part I, many commentators have difficulty in discerning the unity of the entire dissertation. It almost seems as if Kierkegaard completely changes his tone and focus when he mocks the Romantics. But we can detect an underlying coherence that connects the two parts of the book. Throughout Part I, where the focus is on reconstructing what Socrates was like, Kierkegaard emphasizes Socrates' radical negativity. The reason why this negativity (without any positivity) is so central for Kierkegaard is that he sees it as a clue to Socrates' personality, his subjectivity, his inwardness, and his negative freedom. Becoming a human being *begins* with irony – with an experience that emulates Socratic radical negative freedom. I emphasize *begins*, because we discover that there is something fundamentally unstable about irony itself. It can be liberating, but also enslaving and disastrous. Kierkegaard draws out this double-edged, paradoxical character of irony in his characterization of "pure irony."[22] This double-edged, or Janus-faced, character of irony is what unites the two parts of *The Concept of Irony*. As Söderquist notes, "irony can work as a perquisite for authentic selfhood and [as] a temptation which results in the spiritual death of the self" (Söderquist 2013: 87).

After discussing (and critiquing) the varieties of irony as a "figure of speech," Kierkegaard stresses the difference between this common use of irony and irony in its eminent sense. "Irony *sensu eminentiori* [in the eminent sense] is directed not against this or that passing entity but against the entire actuality at a certain time and under certain conditions...It is not this or that phenomenon but the totality of existence *sub specie ironiae* [under the aspect of irony]. To this extent we see the correctness of Hegel's view of irony as infinite absolute negativity" (Kierkegaard 1989: 254). The more one pushes this ironic stance to its extreme, the more it becomes clear that it is unstable and paradoxical. If the ironist is to be thoroughly consistent, he must turn his irony against his own ironic stance. If he affirms his irony, then he is earnest about his irony. But to be earnest about anything is not to be a pure ironist. If he doesn't affirm his irony – and is only an occasional ironist – then he is not a thoroughly consistent ironist. Ironists pay a high price for their disengagement. They lack any continuity in their character, and they become

enslaved by their moods, which leads to boredom. "An ironist poetically composes himself and his environment with the greatest possible poetic license, as he lives in this totally hypothetical and
subjective way, his life loses all continuity" (Kierkegaard 1989: 284).
(Kierkegaard here anticipates the problems of *this* type of ironic
stance that are explored in *Either/Or*.) Andrew Cross articulates the
paradoxical quality of "pure irony."

> The ironist, then, has a nihilistic attitude toward social existence and
> toward all aspects of human life that are immediate and, hence, to be
> held apart from the self. His irony is the manifestation of, and the
> means of preserving, this radical detachment from the putatively pur-
> poseful activities and concerns that constitute social life...
> But what of the ironist's attitude toward himself – that is toward
> the ironic self, the thing that is held apart from the embodied social
> being that it playfully manipulates? Does the ironist identify himself
> with the activity of ironizing, and does he see this activity, the main-
> taining of this orientation, as having some point? Here, it seems, the
> ironist has been backed into a corner. If he does take this way of exist-
> ing seriously, then this irony ceases to be comprehensive; there exists
> one way of life that he does not "negate" or repudiate, namely the
> ironic life. To the extent that this is so, he is not a pure, total, ironist;
> he does not go so far, in his self-disengagement, as to disengage himself
> from his own self-disengaging. (Cross 1998: 138–9)

I have been tracing some of the instabilities, tensions, and paradoxes that Kierkegaard exposes in *The Concept of Irony*. We have seen
how Kierkegaard swerves away from Hegel in his characterization of
Socrates. Socrates exposes the instabilities within the Sophists'
stance, and is more thorough in his destructive negative critique of
tradition, authority, and conventional norms. Unlike Hegel, Kierkegaard claims that Socrates' ignorance is not feigned. He offers us
nothing positive. But we have also seen how Kierkegaard valorizes
Socrates' ironic stance. It is the key for understanding Socrates' personality, his subjectivity, and his inwardness. Even more important,
Socrates exemplifies the playful liberating irony that *begins* a life that
may be called human. As we pursue the concept of "pure irony," we
see how it becomes self-destructive. In Kierkegaard's sharp critique
of Romantic irony, we witness the full force of what he takes to be
the incoherence of "pure irony." The question we need to confront is:
How are we to distinguish liberating irony from enslaving destructive irony?

How are we to discern those features of irony (exemplified by Socrates) that Kierkegaard clearly valorizes – and continued to valorize throughout his life – from those features that he deplores, which are epitomized by the Romantic ironists. I do not think that Kierkegaard resolves this tension in *The Concept of Irony*. He makes a gesture toward resolving it in the final section of his dissertation entitled "Irony as a Controlled Element, the Truth of Irony" – the last six pages of his long book.

What he says here is at once extremely sketchy and elusive. He speaks of controlling irony so that it can "be halted in the wild infinity into which it rushes ravenously"; but he doesn't really indicate how this is to be accomplished. He tells us that "irony as the negative is the way, it is not the truth." But he doesn't tell us precisely how irony is the way, and why the dialectic of irony doesn't end up enslaving us rather than liberating us. He declares that "irony as a controlled element manifests itself in its truth precisely by teaching how to actualize actuality, by placing the appropriate emphasis on actuality" (Kierkegaard 1989: 326–8).

But he doesn't explain what this means or how it is to be achieved. Nor does he enable us to understand how this "actualizing actuality" differs from the positivity that he has so adamantly excluded from his analysis of radical negative irony. When we compare what Kierkegaard says in his very short concluding chapter with his extensive and detailed analysis of Socrates as the ironist, it looks as if Kierkegaard is flatly contradicting himself. He keeps telling us that Socrates has nothing "positive" to offer. Recall how Kierkegaard described what Socrates did with the Sophists. He gave them "the moment in which the momentarily true dissolved into nothing – in other words he let the infinite devour the finite." Socrates' irony "was turned against the whole established order" (Kierkegaard 1989: 213–14). This is why Söderquist speaks of "Kierkegaard's Nihilistic Socrates" (the title of his second chapter) and Cross speaks of the ironist's "nihilistic attitude toward social existence and toward all aspects of human life that are immediate and hence, to be held apart from the self" (Söderquist 2013: 53 and Cross 1998: 138). In the final pages of *The Concept of Irony*, Kierkegaard appears to take back everything that he has insisted upon in his portrayal of Socrates' absolute ironic negativity. Now we are told (instead of radically negating all reality) that we must not hollow out actuality. "[L]ife's content must become a genuine and meaningful element in the higher actuality whose fullness the soul craves" (Kierkegaard 1989: 328). But isn't this really to slip back into a *positivity* that Kierkegaard thoroughly and relentlessly excluded in his depiction of Socrates and when he defined "pure irony"?[23]

The Concept of Irony leaves us in a double bind. To the extent that we accept Kierkegaard's analysis of irony, there seems to be no way to avoid its sheer negativity and self-destruction. To the extent that he softens his analysis and speaks of "controlled irony," he undermines what he has characterized so laboriously as "infinite absolute negativity." Kierkegaard came to appreciate the paradox that he leaves us with at the end of *The Concept of Irony* – and he sought to rethink the meaning of irony. But I do not think that he ever gave up the claim that "no genuinely human life is possible without irony." In *Concluding Unscientific Postscript*, we have an indication of this rethinking when Johannes Climacus asks: "What then is irony if one wants to call Socrates an ironist and does not, like Magister Kierkegaard consciously or unconsciously want to bring out one side?" (Kierkegaard 1992: 503).[24]

Before passing on to how Kierkegaard modifies his understanding of irony, I want to underscore what Kierkegaard preserves from his discussion in *The Concept of Irony* and why he has so emphasized (and exaggerated) Socrates' negativity. The sheer negativity of the ironic stance is an essential *beginning* of the formation of one's own subjectivity and inwardness. One must appropriate and emulate the radical questioning that is characteristic of Socrates. Only by radically questioning the historical and cultural actuality (the prevailing *Sittlichkeit*) within which one finds oneself – whether this be Socrates' Athens or Kierkegaard's nineteenth-century Danish Christendom – can one *begin* to realize a genuinely human life. It is all too easy to deceive oneself, to pretend that one is engaging in radical self-critique when one is really smuggling in unquestioned prejudices and particular beliefs. (This is what the Sophists did. We may call this "the sophistic moment" – wherever and whenever it occurs.) Throughout his life, Kierkegaard was relentless in exposing what he perceived to be the varieties (and pervasiveness) of this type of self-deception. For Kierkegaard, Socrates is an exemplar of negativity, subjectivity, and inwardness. But being an exemplar doesn't mean that we simply honor Socrates as a "hero" or as a "world historical figure." For this becomes a way of *removing* him from ourselves. The really difficult task is to appropriate what Socrates is doing in our *own* lives – to practice for ourselves the radical questioning and negativity that characterize his life. In *Concluding Unscientific Postscript* (with Socrates in mind) Climacus writes:

> Only by paying sharp attention to myself can I come to realize how a historical individuality acted when he was living, and I understand him only when I keep him alive in my understanding and do not, as children do, break the clock in order to understand the life in it, and do not, as speculative thought does, change him into something totally different in order to understand him. *But what it is to live I cannot learn from him as someone dead and gone. I must experience that by myself, and therefore I must understand myself, not the reverse.* (Kierkegaard 1992: 146–7, emphasis added)

These are the words of Climacus, but there is little doubt that they are also the words of Kierkegaard.

But even granting that radical negative freedom is the *beginning* of living a human life, we want to know how to *fulfill* this beginning, how the "truth of irony" is to be realized, how we can move beyond the sheer negativity of irony. We may agree with what Kierkegaard says near the end of *The Concept of Irony*:

> Anyone who does not understand irony at all, who has no ear for its whispering, lacks *eo ipso* [precisely thereby] what could be called *the absolute beginning* of personal life; he lacks the bath of regeneration and rejuvenation, irony's baptism of justification that rescues the soul from having its life in finitude even though it is living energetically and robustly in it. He does not know the refreshment and strengthening that come with undressing when the air gets too hot and heavy and diving him into the sea of irony, not in order to stay here, of course, but in order to come out healthy, happy, and buoyant and to dress again. (Kierkegaard 1989: 326–7, emphasis added)

We want to know how we are to get out of "the sea of irony." How do we get beyond the "absolute beginning of personal life"? We will not find answers in *The Concept of Irony*. To confront these questions, we need to turn to how Kierkegaard (or at least, Climacus) rethinks the meaning and function of irony. Earlier, I introduced Hegel's distinction between abstract negation and determinate negation. At times, Kierkegaard's depiction of Socrates in *The Concept of Irony* comes close to Hegel's understanding of abstract negation. It is empty and results in "pure" nothing. Kierkegaard strongly resists taking the

Hegelian route of determinate negation and mediation. What, then, is the alternative to either empty abstract negation or determinate negation? To discover the answer, we need to turn to Johannes Climacus's depiction of irony.

Moving Beyond "Pure Irony"

In order to pinpoint the place where Kierkegaard rethinks irony, I want to return to Jonathan Lear's description of the "experience of irony." Initially, Lear focuses on the experience of complete disruption and disorientation. Let us recall once again Lear's example of the teacher who experiences a complete "breakdown in *practical intelligibility*" (Lear 2011: 180). The person experiencing *ironic* disruption is not paralyzed. "What is peculiar to irony is that it manifests a *passion for a certain direction*" (Lear 2011: 19, emphasis added). Not surprisingly, this is the very point (and language) that Climacus underscores in his discussion of irony. In the passage just after Climacus criticizes Magister Kierkegaard's one-sided view of irony, he writes: "*Irony is the unity of ethical passion*, which in inwardness infinitely accentuates one's own *I* in relation to the ethical requirement – and culture, which in externality infinitely abstracts from the personal *I* as a finitude included among all the finitudes and particulars" (Kierkegaard 1992: 503, emphasis added). It is this ethical passion that now becomes essential for understanding Socrates as an ironist – and for distinguishing this type of Socratic irony from the radical negativity that culminates in self-destructive "pure irony."[25] The "pure irony" which Kierkegaard characterizes as "infinite absolute negativity" always remains a real possibility. But now we begin to see another possibility, where irony is manifested in ethical passion.[26] Everything depends on which possibility is *actualized* by single individuals. We should recall that in *Philosophical Crumbs* [*Philosophical Fragments*] Climacus describes this movement from possibility to actuality as *freedom*.[27] But Climacus is even more specific. He tells us that "irony is an existence-qualification, and thus nothing is more ludicrous than regarding it as a style of speaking or an author's counting himself lucky to express himself ironically once in a while. The person who has essential irony has it all day long and is not bound to any style, because it is the infinite within him" (Kierkegaard 1992: 503–4).

Irony is a form of life that involves the art of living and is not simply a clever figure of speech. But what precisely does it mean to say that "irony is an existence-qualification"?

> There are three existence-spheres: the aesthetic, the ethical, and the religious. To these there is a respectively corresponding *confinium* (border territory); irony is the *confinium* between the aesthetic and the ethical; humor is the *confinium* between the ethical and the religious. (Kierkegaard 1992: 501–2)[28]

This passage calls for several comments.

First, in distinguishing the three existence-spheres – the aesthetic, the ethical, and the religious – Climacus is reiterating a set of distinctions that Kierkegaard makes in several of his pseudonymous works. There has been a great deal of scholarly debate about the relation of these existence-spheres to each other. One standard view is that they form a type of hierarchy, so that the instability and failures of the aesthetic *inevitably* lead to the ethical, and the instability of the ethical *inevitably* leads to the religious – and finally to faith. I reject this quasi-Hegelian reading of existence-spheres as a progression from the aesthetic through the ethical and ultimately to faith. There is no *necessity* involved in this movement. There is no *compelling reason* (or even psychological condition such as despair) that requires one to move from one existence-sphere to another. This type of dialectical movement is just what Kierkegaard is calling into question. For example, A in *Either/Or* can remain completely unmoved by Judge Wilheim's rhetoric and simply be in his own despair. He need not feel any compulsion to move beyond his aesthetic indulgence: he can even aesthetically "enjoy" his despair. For him there is no meaningful Either/Or as Judge Wilheim defines it, because A does not have a self that has some continuity and stability.

> If you marry, you will regret it, if you do not marry, you will regret it: if you marry or you do not marry, you will regret both. Laugh at the world's follies, you will regret it, weep over them, you will also regret it; if you laugh at the world's follies or if you weep over them, you will regret both. Believe a girl, you will regret it; if you do not believe her, you will also regret it; if you believe a girl or do not believe her, you will regret both. If you hang yourself, you will regret it, if you do not hang yourself, you will also regret it; if you hang yourself or do not hang yourself, you will regret both. This gentlemen, is the sum of all practical wisdom. (Kierkegaard 1992a: 54)

As the judge himself says, it is only when one becomes a self and has chosen the ethical life that an Either/Or makes sense. The movement from the aesthetic to the ethical is a *radically contingent* movement that is not philosophically or psychologically necessitated.[29]

Second, although the three existence-spheres do *not* stand in a progressive hierarchical relationship, there is another question that can be raised about their relationship to each other. To what extent are they really independent of each other? Many of Kierkegaard's texts suggest that we are dealing with three *independent* existence-spheres, but there are many others that suggest a much more complicated interrelationship. In *Either/Or*, Judge William argues that it is only the ethical form of existence that is "truly" aesthetic. And *Either/Or* concludes with the suggestion that the ethical is also religious. At times, Kierkegaard, and his pseudonymous authors, suggest that one can't really lead a genuinely ethical life without being religious – indeed, without being an authentic Christian. For my purposes, I want to bracket the issue of the relationship of ethics, religion, Christianity, and faith (which of course *is central* for Kierkegaard). I want to focus on irony where it is necessary for a life that may be called human. And to become human is to make the transition to what Kierkegaard calls the ethical sphere of existence.

Third, although Climacus doesn't define what he means by a *confinium* in the above passage, we find a helpful characterization of it in *The Concept of Irony*. A *confinium* is a *transitional* element that lies between two things, but "actually belongs neither to the one nor the other" (Kierkegaard 1989: 121). Consequently, if irony is the *confinium* between the aesthetic and the ethical, then we need to understand what is involved in this transition. The idea of a *confinium* as a transitional concept is related to Kierkegaard's insistence that the process of becoming a self (a process that is never completed) is the movement from possibility to actuality. This movement – this *becoming* – is what Kierkegaard calls freedom. "The change of coming into existence is actuality, the transition takes place in freedom" (Kierkegaard 2009: 143). Freedom is manifested in existential choice. It is existential because one is literally choosing how one is to exist, how one is to relate to oneself, to others, and to the world. Such choice is never just a single decisive event. It is a *task* that must be constantly repeated. Of course, as Kierkegaard (and Climacus) point out, there is a minimum sense in which everyone is a self and a human being. This means only that each of us has the capacity (*the possibility*) of *becoming* a self by virtue of existential choice. This possibility, however, may never be freely actualized. We can remain (and Kierkegaard suggests that most of us do remain) living a life playing with possibilities – as does A in the first part of *Either/Or*. What we learn from Climacus is that there are *two* dynamic interrelated moments in becoming human. The first is that moment of absolute infinite negativity in which we distance ourselves from the historical actuality (the *Sittlichkeit*) in which we find ourselves. This is exemplified by Socrates, who did this in a more thorough and consistent manner than anyone before him. But what we learn from *Concluding Unscientific Postscript* is that *if* the ironist does not move beyond this initial stage, then his irony becomes self-defeating, and even self-destructive. It is the Romantic ironist who is never able to get beyond this initial self-destructive stage of irony. What he lacks is the ethical passion that Socrates manifests. The first stage of irony is the *beginning* of subjectivity and inwardness, but this subjectivity and inwardness is empty unless there is the second moment of *ethical passion*.

Is there any outward sign by which we can distinguish the person who is stuck in the first stage of irony – the stage of sheer negativity – and the ironist who has made the transition to becoming an ethicist? If we follow Climacus, the answer is clearly No! From a third-person point of view, one can never be certain whether the ironist one encounters is stuck at the first stage or has made the passionate movement beyond and is becoming an ethicist. "As soon as an observer discovers an ironist, he will be attentive, because it is possible that the ironist is an ethicist. But he can also be fooled, because it is not certain that the ironist is an ethicist" (Kierkegaard 1992: 502). This is one of the many reasons why Kierkegaard rejects the Hegelian dictum that the outer is the inner and the inner is the outer.[30] There is no outward sign to determine when the ironist has made the internal move to become an ethicist (and thereby to *become* a human being). Kierkegaard knows that we are desperately searching for some concrete mark, some criterion that will help us to distinguish the pure ironist from the ironist who exhibits ethical passion. Kierkegaard also knows that, from the speculative (Hegelian) perspective, unless we can conceptually specify some difference that really makes a difference between the pure ironist and the ironical ethicist, we have no *conceptual* basis for claiming that there really is a difference between the two. But this is precisely his point: there are no conceptual criteria for distinguishing these two types of ironist.

Indeed, we can now illuminate the meaning and purpose of indirect communication, as well as what Kierkegaard is doing with his pseudonymous authors. Kierkegaard – and his pseudonymous creations – are teasing and playing with us (his readers) – but it is a deadly serious play. He knows that we desperately want some definite *criteria* that will give us an indication of what we must do to become ethical human beings. And the pseudonymous authors (despite their disclaimers) constantly seduce us, the readers, into thinking that we have something determinate to hold on to.[31] Kierkegaard exposes the multiple ways in which we deceive ourselves about our inwardness and subjectivity. The sad fact is that most of us have "no taste for accentuating the personal *I*" (Kierkegaard 1992: 503). Climacus even tells us that Hegelian ethics is not just mistaken, it is *unethical*. "The desperate attempt of the miscarried Hegelian ethics to make the state into the court of last resort of ethics is a highly unethical attempt to finitize individuals, an unethical flight from the category of individuality to the category of the race" (Kierkegaard 1992: 503).[32] If we rigorously pursue the logic of Kierkegaard's thinking, then we must even be wary of Climacus's claim that Socrates was an ethicist who uses his irony as his incognito – his disguise. And the reason is that we never *can* have access to someone's subjectivity – to the inwardness that infinitely accentuates one's own *I* in relation to the ethical requirement.

With this revised understanding of irony, we can return to the final section of *The Concept of Irony*, and read it in a new light. It is entitled "Irony as a Controlled Element, the Truth of Irony." From the perspective of Kierkegaard's later understanding of irony, it is misleading and awkward to speak of irony as "controlled." It is more accurate to speak of the movement *beyond* pure irony – the existential movement that involves ethical passion. The reason why it is misleading to speak of "controlled" irony is that this sounds as if we are limiting the function of irony. But I don't think that Kierkegaard wants to limit the first stage of irony – the moment in which one negates and isolates oneself from one's immediate historical actuality. Extreme negative freedom is a necessary condition for becoming human, becoming a self. It can be both liberating and terrifying. And it can be *self-destructive* if one doesn't move beyond this first stage. The "truth of irony" becomes manifest only in the erotic movement beyond this first stage – in the ethical passion manifested in becoming a human being. It is this movement – this *becoming* – that was *not* really clarified in *The Concept of Irony*. This is why it looks as if Kierkegaard is backsliding when he emphasizes the positive freedom of controlled irony. Now we can make sense of what Magister Kierkegaard is affirming: "Irony as the negative is the way; it is not the truth but the way" (Kierkegaard 1989: 327). The truth of irony is making the *transition* beyond this first unstable stage of irony. There is a longing, an *Eros*, a passion that transforms us. Actuality, we are told, "acquires its validity through action." But this action is an *internal* movement – intensifying one's subjectivity and inwardness. "[L]ife's content must become a genuine and meaningful element in a higher actuality whose fullness the soul craves" (Kierkegaard 1989: 328). I interpret this as meaning that after radically isolating oneself from the world (the first moment of irony as negative freedom), one can return to actuality in a new way.[33] The difference that makes all the difference is an *invisible* and *silent* one. It is the difference that results from the unseen ethical passion and *Eros*, the passion and *Eros* that one must directly *experience* to become a human being, the personal existential activity by which one deepens one's subjectivity and inwardness, and thereby transforms mere "negative" irony into something "positive."

Consequently, we are left with a paradox (not the Absolute Paradox) of indirect communication. No one can tell us how to make the existential choices in becoming a self. Indeed, no one can provide us with even conceptual guidelines about how to do this. Here we can return to the question of Socrates and Socratic irony. The paradox of Socrates is not that his ignorance is feigned, but rather that it is *genuine*. There is no definitive indication that Socrates is really capable of answering the questions that he constantly presses in his elenctic encounters with others. And there is no convincing evidence that these encounters enable his interlocutors to lead more virtuous lives. Many of them (like Alcibiades, Critias, and Charmides) turn out to be tyrants. At the same time, Plato presents Socrates as living a just, moderate, courageous, and wise life – without ever telling us precisely how Socrates managed to do this. We think of him as an *ideal* being who is not quite human and not quite divine (like his *daimon*). In doing so, we *remove* him from ourselves – and go about our normal business. At this point we might recall Nehamas's description of the Socratic dialogues: "The Socratic dialogues demand of their audience what Socrates asks of his interlocutors: to examine their own beliefs on any subject of importance to them, to determine to what other beliefs they are logically related, to accept only those that are compatible with one another, and *to live their lives accordingly*. That is a question we are as good at ignoring as any of Socrates' simple interlocutors" (Nehamas 1998: 42, emphasis added).

I suggest that something similar is characteristic of Kierkegaard's writings – both the pseudonymous writings *and* those that bear the signature "Søren Kierkegaard." A great deal of scholarly ink has been spilt over the question of who is the "real" Kierkegaard, what were his "real" beliefs, what writings can we take as being authoritative. But, as I read Kierkegaard, this is the *wrong* question to ask. It is not just that there are masks behind masks – even when Kierkegaard professes to speak from his "point of view."[34] The difficult question that Kierkegaard and all the pseudonymous authors want *each of us* to confront is: How am *I* to become a self?[35] This is a question that cannot be answered conceptually. Nor can anyone answer it for me. I answer it only through my own existential choices, my ethical passion, and my individual freedom. "[W]e have forgotten that an achievement is worthless if it is not made one's own" (Kierkegaard 1989: 327). This is why to become human or to learn what it means to be human does not come that easily. Climacus tells us that "The great merit of the Socratic was precisely to emphasize that the knower is an existing person and that to exist is the essential" (Kierkegaard 1992: 207). If we take Socrates as the ethicist who manifests the unity of ethical passion as some sort of hero or ideal exemplar, this *can* become a way of removing him from ourselves. This is just another trap – another evasion. In one of his journal entries, Kierkegaard writes:

So if an ethical man finds that people admire him...he must himself see that this holds a deception, an untruth. An ethical man must not let people admire him, but – through him – they must be urged toward the Ethical. As soon as people are permitted to admire an ethical man they elevate him into a genius, i.e. put him on a different plane, and *ethically*, that very thing constitutes the most horrible fallacy, for *the ethical shall and must be universally human*. An ethical man must constantly maintain, and inculcate in others, that *every human being* is as capable [of ethical conduct] as he. So there we have a different relationship. Instead of laying claim to admiration (which people are not so unwilling to give, particularly if it suits their indolence for instance by saying: Well, it's easy for him; he is a genius, etc.) he demands *existence* from them: practice what you preach. That makes them angry. They wanted to admire him in order to be rid of him (i.e. the gadfly-sting of his existence) but the human feeling in him that makes him say: anybody can do it as well as I – calls forth hatred and makes people wish to have him at a distance. (Kierkegaard 1960: 113–14, emphasis added)

Finally, I want to return to what I have called Kierkegaard's swerve from Hegel. In Hegel's account of negativity, there is also a grand Either/Or: *either* sheer negativity that results in emptiness and nothingness, *or* determinate negation that results in mediation and universality. It is the iterated forms of determinate negation that are the essence of systematic speculative philosophy. In *The Concept of Irony*, Kierkegaard *resists* the Hegelian doctrine of determinate negation. But in his appropriation of Hegel's notion of infinite absolute negation, he seems to characterize Socrates as the ironist who epitomizes the sheer negativity that leads to emptiness. This is the portrayal of Socrates as a thoroughgoing nihilist. Consequently, Magister Kierkegaard seems to be caught in the Hegelian Either/Or. He rejects determinate negation – which leaves him with the alternative of empty negativity. Yet Kierkegaard radically swerves away from the Hegelian Either/Or. This is anticipated in *The Concept of Irony*, but becomes clear in *Concluding Unscientific Postscript*. Kierkegaard (and Climacus) reject the way in which Hegel *frames* the alternatives of this Either/Or. There is another way besides sheer emptiness or the seduction of determinate negation. This is Kierkegaard's swerve to ethical passion: freely choosing what we are to become. This is no longer sheer negativity; but neither is it mediation and determinate negation. Rather, it is learning *how* to exist, learning what is involved in becoming a human being, learning – that is, *choosing – how* to live one's life. And with this we have a new and different Either/Or. One can stay frozen at the stage of sheer negativity. There is no necessity or compelling reason to move beyond this – even if it results in despair and melancholy. But it is possible for each of us as "single individuals" to *freely* actualize ourselves as ethical human beings, and thereby move beyond the unstable negativity of pure irony.[36]

Chapter 4

Irony, Philosophy, and Living a Human Life

In this final chapter, I want to integrate what we have learnt about how irony is related to living a human life. To set the context for my reflections, I return to the distinction that Nehamas introduces between philosophy as a theoretical discipline and philosophy as a practical discipline. Philosophers from the time of classical Greece have been concerned with *both* theoretical and practical questions (and their relation to each other). The very distinction between *theoria* and *praxis* has come down to us from the Greeks. Despite the many historical transformations of the meaning of these expressions, and the different positions developed by philosophers concerning them, some version of a theoretical/practical distinction is as fundamental today as it was in classical Greece.

But Nehamas has something more specific in mind in introducing this distinction. He calls attention to different *types* of philosophizing. The theoretical type is one in which we are primarily interested in getting things right and trying to ascertain what is objectively true – and we do this by presenting the strongest arguments and justifications for the theses that we advance. Anything may be treated in this theoretical manner, including such practical disciplines as ethics and politics. Although the origins of the theoretical style are as old as philosophy itself, there is a specific sense in which philosophy has become primarily a theoretical discipline in our time. Today, insofar as philosophy is a professional academic discipline, the theoretical style has become so dominant that many philosophers scarcely recognize any alternative – and even think (anachronistically) that philosophy has always been such a theoretical discipline. But this contemporary bias ignores a tradition that can also be traced back to the Greeks. The primary purpose of this other philosophical tradition is to make a difference in how we live our lives. Gaining theoretical knowledge of the cosmos and our place in the cosmos is for the purpose of achieving concrete practical wisdom. As Nehamas notes, even when Aristotle identified philosophy with *theoria*, at the end of the *Nicomachean Ethics*, his main purpose was to argue "that a *life* of theoretical activity, the life of philosophy was the best life the human beings could lead" (Nehamas 1998: 2). Without denying the importance of theoretical reflection in ancient philosophy, Pierre Hadot has emphasized the extent to which ancient philosophy involved a vision – and specific *practices* required for a certain way of living in the world: "Philosophical discourse, then, originates in a choice of life and an existential option – not vice versa" (Hadot 2002: 3). This distinction between philosophy as a theoretical discipline and philosophy as a practical way of life is over-simplified, especially when used to distinguish ancient from modern philosophy. We can see this vividly in the case of Descartes, who is frequently (especially in textbook versions of the history of philosophy) taken to be the "father" of modern philosophy. There is a long tradition, still very much alive in contemporary philosophy, of treating Descartes as a paradigmatic theoretical philosopher concerned with basic metaphysical and epistemological issues.

> The *Meditations* has been read as the great rationalist treatise of modern times. Its potentially radical implications have inspired many, because of Descartes' demand that we should not rely on unfounded opinions, prejudices, tradition, or external authority, but only upon the authority of reason itself. Few philosophers since Descartes have accepted his substantive claims, but there can be little doubt that the problems, metaphors, and questions that he bequeathed to us have been at the very center of philosophy since Descartes – problems concerning the foundations of knowledge and the sciences, mind–body dualism, our knowledge of the "external" world, how the mind "represents" the world, the nature of consciousness, thinking, and will, whether physical reality is to be understood as a grand mechanism, and how this is compatible with human freedom. Philosophers have been primarily concerned with the precise character and cogency of Descartes' *arguments*. (Bernstein 1983: 16–17)

But there is another way of reading the *Meditations*, although this is rarely considered by professional philosophers, and is much closer to the tradition of philosophy as a way of life.

> The *Meditations* portrays a journey of the soul, a meditative reflection on human finitude, through which we gradually deepen our understanding of what it really means to be limited, finite creatures who are completely dependent on an all-powerful, beneficent, perfect, and infinite God. If we practice these spiritual exercises earnestly, as Descartes urges us to do, if we follow the precarious stages of this journey without losing our way, then we discover that this is a journey that is at once terrifying and liberating, culminating in the calm reassurance that although we are eminently fallible and subject to all sorts of contingencies, we can rest secure in the deepened self-knowledge that we are creatures of a beneficent God who has created us in his image. The terrifying quality of this journey is reflected in the allusions to madness, darkness, the dread of waking from a self-deceptive dream world, the fear of having "all of a sudden fallen into very deep water" where "I can neither make certain of setting my feet on the bottom, nor can I swim and so support myself on the surface," and the anxiety of imagining that I may be nothing more than a plaything of an all-powerful evil demon. But the more I probe my finitude and realize how completely dependent I am on a beneficent God, for he sustains me at every moment of my existence, the more I can be liberated from this dread, fear, and anxiety. It is a spiritual journey that culminates with the assurance that I can and ought to "set aside all the doubts of these past few days as hyperbolical and ridiculous… For because God is in no wise a deceiver, it follows that I am not deceived in this. But because the exigencies of action often oblige us to make up our minds before having leisure to examine matters carefully we must confess that the life of man is very frequently subject to error in respect to individual objects, and we must in the end acknowledge the infirmity of our nature." (Bernstein 1983: 17–18)[1]

I have sketched two different readings of the *Meditations* for several reasons. First, the distinction between the two different conceptions of philosophy that Nehamas describes does not easily align (as Nehamas himself stresses) with the distinction between ancient and modern philosophy. We find the legacy of the tradition of philosophy concerned with how to live one's life in philosophers throughout the history of philosophy, including Hume, Kant, Hegel, Nietzsche, James, Heidegger, Foucault, and Wittgenstein. This is not to deny that, among professional academic philosophers today, some version of what Nehamas calls theoretical philosophy is dominant. Second, although there are different types of philosophizing, theoretical and practical orientations are intimately interrelated and interdependent. We see this even when we consider some of the clearest examples of the practice of philosophy as a way of life. In the various Hellenistic schools that arose in the late fourth century BCE, it is evident that their different conceptions of how to live one's life are based upon their views of the nature of the cosmos, the physical universe, and what we can and cannot know and control. Even if we agree with Hadot that the differing physical and epistemological theories of these schools were intended to support their "spiritual" goals, it is still essential to pay attention to, and evaluate, the theoretical claims that inform their understanding of self-transformation.

The contemporary philosophers whom I have discussed – Lear, Rorty, Vlastos, and Nehamas (I also include myself) – work within the theoretical discipline of philosophy. We are all professors of philosophy, and our writings are judged by the prevailing standards of the philosophical profession. Except for occasional supplementary biographical statements, our colleagues and readers have no interest in how we live our lives. Yet each of us has been concerned to do justice to the other subterranean tradition in philosophy. This is what motivates exploration of the role of irony in living a human life. I do not think that the reason for this has anything to do with a nostalgia for an idealized past that is lost. Rather, it has more to do with a perceived lack of balance. We are still deeply affected by the image of Socrates, the ironist who, despite his claim to ignorance, managed to live a just, temperate, and courageous life. He is not wise (only the gods are wise), but the exemplar of the lover of wisdom – a wisdom concretely manifested in his everyday life.

To dramatize the issue of what philosophical thinking has to do with how one lives a life, we need think only of the case of Heidegger. Heidegger (along with Wittgenstein) dedicated his philosophical life to criticizing the theoretical style of philosophizing – what Heidegger called "the onto-theological" tradition. Many have taken Heidegger's concern with "thrownness," "anxiety," "authenticity," and "care" as indications of him calling us back to the tradition of philosophy as the art of living. But with the revelations of his longstanding identification with the Nazis, his dubious ethical behavior during the Nazi period, his anti-Semitic remarks, and his refusal to make an unambiguous statement condemning the Holocaust, serious questions have been raised about Heidegger as a person and his philosophy. Reactions have been extreme.[2] There are those who condemn Heidegger outright and claim that his offensive Nazi views are deeply embedded in his philosophical views; and there are those who want to draw a distinction between the outstanding brilliance of his philosophy and his "unfortunate" personal behavior and remarks. Passions and polemic run high, whatever view one takes toward Heidegger and his philosophical writings. My point in raising the Heidegger question here is *not* to enter the fray, but rather to indicate how this debate compels us to ask questions about the relation of philosophy to living one's life – about the relation of philosophical thinking to concrete embodied practical judgment. And what does this have to do with ironic existence?

The Art of Living

The four contemporary philosophers whom I have discussed – Lear, Rorty, Vlastos, and Nehamas – are all concerned with the tradition of philosophy as an art of living that involves concrete practices. Let me begin by reconsidering Vlastos, a paradigmatic theoretical philosopher (in Nehamas's sense), whose primary focus was to provide the evidence and the arguments for understanding Socrates and what is distinctive about Socratic irony. His thesis, as we recall, is that Socrates transformed *eirōneia* (with its negative connotation of intentional deception) into *ironia*. *Ironia* ("irony") is "speech used to express a meaning that runs contrary to what is said – the perfect medium for mockery innocent of deceit" (Vlastos 1991: 28). Socrates' ironical utterances exhibit "complex irony" – the type of irony such that "what is said both is and isn't what is meant" (Vlastos 1991: 31). But Vlastos makes a much more ambitious claim about Socrates: that Socrates brought about this change in the meaning of irony because he created a new form of life that he realized in himself. Socrates became the incarnation of the ironist. Socrates, by the force of his personality, transformed *eirōneia* into *ironia*. Consequently, Vlastos underscores the significance of the art of living in transforming philosophical thinking. Although Vlastos and Kierkegaard have radically different conceptions of Socratic irony, it is striking that both emphasize that Socrates created something new through his personality, which has inspired thinkers ever since. In *The Concept of Irony*, Kierkegaard keeps emphasizing the distinctiveness of Socrates' ironic personality. The fascination with Socrates' "ironic existence" (to use Lear's expression) is just as deep in Nehamas, Rorty, and Lear. Despite their differences, each of them thinks of Socrates as a figure who transcends his historical context and becomes an inspiration for how to live a human life.

Let us consider some of the key differences among these thinkers and whether their differences can (or cannot) be reconciled. I have already commented on a tension in Vlastos's analysis of Socratic irony. On the one hand, he stresses the significance of Socrates as the paradigmatic *eirōn* who created a new form of life. On the other hand, when Vlastos claims that "what is said both is and isn't what is meant: its surface content is meant to be true in one sense, false in another" (Vlastos 1991: 31), he comes close to banalizing the meaning of Socratic irony. In fairness to Vlastos, it should be noted that there are many instances of irony in the Socratic dialogues that appear to fit his description of complex irony. On the surface, what Socrates says is true, but we can ascertain another sense in which what he says is false. (Sometimes what appears to be false turns out to be true.) Vlastos claims that "the great philosophical paradoxes of which we hear in Plato's earlier dialogues, like Socrates' disavowal of knowledge and of teaching," are instances of complex irony (Vlastos 1991: 32). To justify his claim, Vlastos *explicitly* states the senses in which Socrates does and does not have knowledge, as well as the senses in which Socrates is and is not a teacher. This leads him to a controversial (and I think dubious) interpretation of these instances of alleged complex irony. When Socrates claims that he does not have knowledge, Vlastos says he wants to assure "his hearers that in the moral domain there is not a single proposition that he claims to know with *certainty*" (Vlastos 1991: 32, emphasis added). This is the sense in which Socrates' profession of his ignorance is *true*. But the reason why Socrates' disavowal of knowledge exemplifies complex irony is because there is another sense in which the claim to ignorance is *false*. This is the sense of "knowledge" that is "justified true belief." By "justified true belief" (applied to Socrates), Vlastos means the type of belief that is "justifiable through the peculiarly Socratic method of elenctic argument" (Vlastos 1991: 32). According to Vlastos, if a thesis withstands the examination of elenctic argument, it is a justifiable true belief. This is the sense in which Socrates *does* have "knowledge"

– that is, justified true belief. So what initially seems paradoxical turns out not to be paradoxical at all, but rather an instance of complex irony.[3]

I find Vlastos's dissolution of the "paradox" of Socrates' disavowal of knowledge unpersuasive for several reasons. The distinction between knowing with certainty and justified true belief was not entirely novel in Attic Greece (even though the expression "justified true belief" has become a term of art only in contemporary epistemology). Something like this distinction appears in many of Plato's dialogues (and is indeed fundamental to his account of knowledge in the *Republic*, especially the image of the divided line). If the point of Socrates' disavowal of knowledge is simply a way of indicating that, although he doesn't have certain knowledge, he does have justified true belief, then why doesn't Plato have Socrates say this directly? What is the point of the irony? It would seem to be an elaborate (and apparently misleading) device to make a perfectly straightforward point. Vlastos might respond that the point of the irony is to get his interlocutors to grasp this distinction *for themselves*. But do we need complex irony to grasp that there is a distinction between knowledge that we claim to be certain and the type of "knowledge" that is only "justified true belief"? I don't think there is textual evidence to support the belief that any of Socrates' interlocutors grasp this distinction (for themselves) *because* of Socrates' elenctic arguments.

There are also further scholarly difficulties with Vlastos's distinction between two different conceptions of knowledge. By "justified true belief" in the context of the early dialogues, Vlastos means the "knowledge" that is justifiable through the Socratic method of elenctic argument. Charles Kahn nicely summarizes what Vlastos means by elenctic knowledge: "By elenctic knowledge, Vlastos means moral conviction based upon repeated success in exposing weakness and contradiction in the views of dissenting interlocutors" (Kahn 1992: 244). Kahn also says: "It is, I suggest, this concept of elenctic knowledge that forms the key to Vlastos's reconstruction of the Socratic (or early Platonic) philosophy as a unified whole, not only distinct from but opposed to the philosophy of the middle dialogues" (Kahn 1992: 244). I agree with Kahn that Vlastos's understanding of "elenctic knowledge" is the key for his distinction of "two" Socrates in the Platonic dialogues *and* the key for understanding Vlastos's claim that complex irony enables us to "solve" the paradox of Socrates' disavowal of knowledge. Kahn develops a systematic (and in my judgment, a devastating) critique of Vlastos's analysis of elenctic knowledge as well as of Vlastos's claim that elenchus is the exclusive and distinctive method of the early Platonic dialogues.[4] We don't need to review the details of Kahn's critique.[5] For my purpose, it is sufficient to note that if there are serious scholarly questions (as indeed there are) about Vlastos's characterization of elenctic argument and knowledge, then consequently, there are serious doubts about the correctness of Vlastos's thesis that the appeal to what is "known" by elenctic argument provides the "solution" to the paradox of Socrates' disavowal of knowledge.[6] Similar problems arise concerning Vlastos's claims about Socrates as a teacher. There is little doubt that Socrates does not simply transfer knowledge to a learner's mind. In this conventional sense, Socrates is *not* a teacher, and his denial that he is a teacher is *true*. But in what sense is Socrates a teacher? Vlastos tells us:

> But in the sense which *he* [Socrates] would give to "teaching" – engaging would-be learners in elenctic argument to make them aware of their own ignorance and *enable them to discover for themselves the truth that the teacher had held back* – in that sense of "teaching" Socrates would want to say that he is a teacher, the only true teacher; his dialogue with his fellows *is meant to have, and does have, the effect of evoking and assisting their own effort at moral self-improvement*." (Vlastos 1991: 32, emphasis added)

Something like this is frequently said about Socrates as a moral teacher. But there are problems with this account. Is there any clear evidence that any of Socrates' interlocutors "discover for themselves the truth that the teacher had held back"? What precisely is this *truth*? Although Socrates' interlocutors frequently admit their mistakes, there is no *unambiguous* evidence that these elenctic encounters result in "their own effort at moral self-improvement."[7]

Vlastos begins *Socrates: Ironist and Moral Philosopher* by speaking about Socrates' "strangeness." This is the keynote of Alcibiades' famous speech in the *Symposium* that begins: "Such is his strangeness that you will search and search among those living now and among men of the past, and never come close to what he is himself and to the things he says (221D)" (Vlastos 1991: 1).[8] But Vlastos's description of Socratic irony does not capture the strangeness of Socrates. His analysis of Socratic irony as complex irony is a bit too pat. This is the key point of Nehamas's critique of Vlastos. Nehamas shows that Socrates is far more strange, mysterious, opaque, and ambiguous than Vlastos indicates. For Nehamas, the genius of Plato is to have created a character who is at once opaque, but at the same time intriguing and fascinating – so much so that throughout the ages he has inspired and continues to inspire ever new interpretations. Vlastos's primary motivation in telling us that Socrates created something new when he created complex irony is to defend Socrates against the charge that he is intentionally deceiving his interlocutors. But I agree with Nehamas that the binary opposition between intentional deceit and truthfulness is too simple to capture what Socrates says and does. Although Vlastos acknowledges that Socratic irony involves concealment, I agree with Nehamas that Socrates' concealment is something very different from either lying or truthfulness; "concealment cannot, even when irony is detected, lead us to the ironists' real meaning" (Nehamas 1998: 62). For Vlastos, the question of Socratic irony poses a problem that can be solved by making clear the distinctions between what Socrates knows and does not know, and between how he teaches and does not teach. This understanding of complex irony requires that we specify a *determinate* sense of what is true and what is false in an ironic figure of speech. For Nehamas, this approach to Socratic irony flattens out Socrates' strangeness and misses what is distinctive about Socratic irony – namely, Socrates' silence. Initially it may seem (as Nehamas acknowledges) hyperbolic to speak of Socrates' silence. But Nehamas wants to emphasize the *opacity* of Socrates. We, the readers of the early Platonic dialogues, can never quite pin down what Socrates knows and doesn't know. His ignorance is not feigned – at least, not feigned in the sense that there are *truths* that Socrates clearly *knows*, which he is not revealing to his interlocutors (except, of course, the "knowledge" of his ignorance and lack of wisdom). Or, more precisely, if there are such truths that Socrates knows, they are never explicitly revealed. Irony doesn't consist in saying the contrary of what one means, but rather in saying something different. Socrates, then, is an enigma or a riddle, but not the type of enigma that can be solved once and for all (unlike Alan Turing's enigma). That is why the figure of Socrates and his use of irony invite – indeed *provoke* – endless interpretation.[9] As I have suggested, in Derrida's terms, there is something intrinsically "undecidable" about Socratic irony.

As we have seen, what is especially intriguing about Socratic irony is that, even on Vlastos's account, it is not exclusively a figure of speech. Socrates is the "incarnation" (Vlastos's expression) of irony; this is the way he lived his life. This is the aspect of Socratic irony that Nehamas rightly underscores. Socrates initiates the tradition of philosophy as the art of living, where what one professes and the way one lives one's life have a direct and intimate bearing on one another. Here too there is an enigma – but not the type of enigma for which there is a clear solution. We are never quite told how Socrates managed this – how he managed to live a virtuous life – but nevertheless professed his ignorance of the knowledge of virtue. Socrates becomes the exemplar of the lover of wisdom whose thinking and acting form a seamless whole. But this doesn't mean that we can become like him by trying to imitate him. Rather, as Kierkegaard stresses, we must seek to live our *own* lives – as "single individuals" in society – in a way that emulates and is inspired by the type of questioning and self-examination that Socrates practiced. And this is not only difficult, but it is also risky.

Lear agrees with some features of Nehamas's understanding of irony, but – in the main – he sharply disagrees with his approach. Like Nehamas, Lear stresses that irony is intimately involved in how individuals live their lives. But Lear distances himself from Nehamas (and Vlastos) for several reasons. He accuses them both of mistakenly focusing on irony as a figure of speech.[10] For Lear (following his interpretation of Kierkegaard), this is a secondary, derivative form of irony that presupposes the first-personal, present tense experience of irony. Unlike Nehamas, Lear does not think that Socrates is completely inscrutable or that it is impossible to peer into the ironist's mind. On the contrary, Lear claims to know *precisely* what Socrates is thinking when he stands silently all night on the battlefield at Potidaea. But the distinctive feature of Lear's approach to irony is that he highlights an aspect of irony (and Socratic irony) that receives little attention from either Vlastos or Nehamas – the disorienting, disruptive, uncanny aspect of the experience of irony. Despite the criticisms that I raised about Lear's conception of irony, he makes an important contribution that enriches our understanding of how irony can *transform* how we live our lives. Unless there is a serious ironic disruption, we will never be provoked into the radical right-hand questioning that is required for undergoing the *transformative* experience of irony. The experience of irony involves a desire – *Eros* – that motivates us to seek to close the gap between our practical identities and the aspirations that are implicit in them. This may lead to developing the capacity for irony – the capacity to occasion an experience of irony (in oneself or another). And if we are lucky, we can turn this capacity into "ironic existence" – a human excellence – "the capacity for deploying irony in the right way at the right time in the living of a distinctively human life." This is why Lear agrees with Kierkegaard that "it is ironic existence that is the not-that-easy of becoming human" (Lear 2011: 9).

At this point, it is helpful to distinguish among first-person, second-person, and third-person aspects of irony. Typically, we think of irony as taking place between a speaker and a hearer (even in a written text). For example, when we consider Socrates' ironic remarks, we initially focus on the exchange with the person whom he is addressing – and the effects of Socrates' remarks. For example, when Euthyphro firmly declares that he has accurate knowledge of piety and impiety, Socrates says that he is eager to become Euthyphro's pupil. Given Euthyphro's obtuseness, we are amused that Euthyphro appears to be completely oblivious to Socrates' irony. Although this exchange takes place between two persons in a Platonic dialogue, we can also discern how first-person and third-person aspects are involved. To claim that Socrates' statement is an ironic remark (and not a straightforward assertion), we must ascribe to Socrates the intent to be ironic. When Vlastos defends his thesis that Socratic irony is "complex irony," he focuses on what he takes to be Socrates' first-personal *intention*. For Nehamas, establishing what is Socrates' intention is far more ambiguous and difficult. We might say that Socrates' intention is expressed and revealed in what he says and does (not in some postulated mental state that precedes his action).

Nehamas's interpretation of Platonic irony (as distinguished from Socratic irony) is a good example of the priority of a third-person ironic perspective. What is Plato doing in the *Euthyphro* when he creates a character as obtuse, self-deceived, and arrogant as Euthyphro? Plato's irony is directed at *us* (the third-person readers of the dialogue). We may feel superior to Euthyphro; we may laugh at him as a comic figure; we may even go about our business after reading the dialogue just as Euthyphro proposes to do. "Socrates' irony is directed at Euthyphro only as a means; its real goal are the readers of Plato's dialogue" (Nehamas 1998: 41).

Suppose we accept Nehamas's interpretation of Plato's goal in writing the *Euthyphro* and ask what it takes to experience the sting of Plato's irony. What would be a proper ironic response to the *Euthyphro*? This is where Lear's approach to irony is illuminating. It is always possible to miss the point of an ironic speech act – and indeed, most of Socrates' interlocutors appear to do this. (And if Nehamas is right about Platonic irony, most readers of the dialogues miss Plato's point.) If irony is to be actually *experienced*, then it must be first-personal. Ironical figures of speech are *felicitous* – to use John Austin's expression – only when they provoke the *experience of irony*, the experience of uncanny disruption and disorientation that elicits right-hand questioning and manifests a passion for a new direction. Consequently, Lear enables us to understand how irony must be directly experienced if it is to have a *transformative* effect on how I live my life.

I have argued that there are serious problems with Lear's "radically first-personal, present-tense" approach to irony. Strictly speaking, this experience of irony has nothing to do with ironic speech (either verbal or written). Ironic speech is neither necessary nor sufficient to provoke this experience of irony. Because Lear is so committed to this "radically first-personal present-tense" experience as the *sine qua non* of irony, he ascribes this uncanny disruptive first-personal experience to the originator of irony, Socrates. Socrates' standing still all night silently on the battlefield of Potidaea is "the practical manifestation of his understanding of his own ignorance. It is a form of self-knowledge" (Lear 2011: 85). Lear acknowledges that he is interpreting Socrates' behavior in a controversial manner, but he claims that his interpretation (unlike most other interpretations) makes clear "the philosophical significance" of Socrates' silence. I find this claim dubious.

There is another aspect of Lear's discussion of irony that is insightful, although it also raises all sorts of problems. To appreciate irony, one must have an "ear for irony." Attempting to specify the necessary and sufficient conditions that give rise to the experience of irony is a hopeless task. But then, how does one acquire "an ear for irony"? How does one get the "hang of it"? And how does one "instill" irony? The closest Lear comes to answering these questions is to tell us that we might learn this from the two great ironists Socrates and Kierkegaard. "We learn how to live with irony appropriately by learning from those who are already living an ironic existence" (Lear 2011: 32). But, of course, this means (as Lear acknowledges) that we must grasp what is distinctive about these ironists – and this presupposes that we already have an "ear for irony." This isn't as perplexing as it may initially seem. We can think of analogous instances in which we do say something like this. There are people who are literally or figuratively "tone deaf" to the power of music. Unless one has an "ear for music," one may never be able to appreciate the power and beauty of Beethoven's late piano sonatas. And, as in the case of irony, it seems futile to try to state necessary and sufficient conditions for a musical ear for listening to great classical musical compositions (or even hip hop music). Occasionally, we can help to cultivate an "ear for music," although there are no guarantees that we will succeed. But the issue of having an "ear for irony" becomes a major problem for anyone who claims that experiencing irony is essential for living a human life.

Lear is clearly on to something important when he raises skeptical doubts about the very possibility of giving necessary and sufficient conditions for the occurrence of irony. At one extreme, there are lots of examples where there is little doubt that a remark is ironical in what Lear calls the "routine" understanding of irony. Consider Vlastos's example of "simple and banal" irony. "A British visitor, landing in Los Angeles in the midst of a downpour, is heard to remark, 'What fine weather you are having here'. The weather is foul, he calls it 'fine', and has no trouble making himself understood to mean the contrary of what he says" (Vlastos 1991: 21). I suspect most normal adults would not have any difficulty in grasping the humor of this simple case of irony. Just as there are clear cases of irony where one does not need a refined "ear for irony," so too there are many instances of straightforward literal statements that no one would take as ironical. Unless the author is being playful, we do not read the assertions in a text on mathematics or neurobiology as being ironical. The problems arise somewhere between these banal extremes – especially, for example, in the enigmatic and perplexing remarks of Socrates. Rorty suggests that the permanent fascination with Plato is because, even after millennia of commentary, no one can figure out which passages in the dialogues are jokes. The same can be said about which of Socrates' (and Plato's) remarks are ironical. This uncertainty has led to the most vehement debates about the interpretation of the dialogues. Entire traditions of interpretation center on this issue. For example, Leo Strauss, and many of his students, claim to discover irony in Plato's dialogues where many others see the straightforward advancement of philosophical and political theses.[11] Frequently, we don't know if something we hear or read is ironical (and in what sense it is ironical). There is an ineradicable indeterminacy about many instances of irony. Even a first-personal report about the experience of irony may be inconclusive, confused, or mistaken. When someone questions whether a remark, a text – or even a first-personal experience – is ironical, it is relevant to ask: What are the reasons for making this claim? We enter what Wilfrid Sellars called the "logical space of reasons." The reasons marshalled may be (and frequently are) contested – as they have been in the claims about Platonic and Socratic irony. In short, although there is something right about Lear's claim about an "ear for irony" and his insistence on the first-personal character of the experience of irony, specific instances of alleged irony can *always* be contested. Then what is required is some sort of argument to show that what one *takes* to be ironical *really* is ironical. Disputes about what is and isn't ironical may not be resolvable.

What does Rorty contribute to our understanding of irony – especially to the role of irony for living a human life? Initially, I want to emphasize Rorty's deflationary approach. He eschews the idea that there is an *essential core* to human life. Rorty doesn't pretend to tell us what irony "really is." His proposal is much more modest – but no less important. He *stipulates* what he means by "the ironist" in order to sketch the figure of the "liberal ironist," and he describes this in a way that makes it as attractive as possible. When discussing Rorty's intellectual development, I stressed how he became increasingly skeptical about *all* foundational philosophical claims. This is especially relevant to his description of final vocabularies – the words we use tell "the story of our lives" (Rorty 1989: 73). Philosophers from Plato to the present purport to tell us what is objectively true, and seek to back up their claims with rationally compelling arguments. Much of Rorty's writing has been directed to ironically exposing what he takes to be the *illusion* of noncircular rational justification in philosophy. This is one of the several reasons why Rorty's critics think of him as a "bad relativist." I have suggested that Rorty is really much closer to Nietzsche and Kierkegaard, who also mock philosophical appeals to rational justification. But, unlike Nietzsche and Kierkegaard, Rorty is a passionate liberal who thinks that cruelty and humiliation are the worst things that we can do. Rorty contrasts "the ironist" with "the metaphysician": "[T]he metaphysician is someone who takes the question 'What is the intrinsic nature of (e.g. justice, science, knowledge, Being, faith, morality, philosophy?' at face value. He assumes that the presence of a term in his own final vocabulary ensures that it refers to something which *has* a real essence" (Rorty 1989: 74).[12] In this broad (and idiosyncratic) characterization of "the metaphysician," Rorty is fully aware that most liberals (past and present), including John Stuart Mill, John Rawls, and Jürgen

Habermas, have been "metaphysicians" – despite all the talk about being post-metaphysical. They believe that their liberal understanding of justice and human rights can be rationally justified (that is, justified by noncircular arguments). And they believe that it is the task of a philosophical theory of justice and human rights to provide such a justification. But Rorty claims that it is no longer viable to hold such a view. This is why he introduces his conception of the ironist. Succinctly stated, the ironist is fully aware of the historical contingency of her final vocabulary.

Strictly speaking, recognizing this contingency is not sufficient for identifying the "ironist." One may grant the historical contingency of a final vocabulary and, at the same time, maintain that it can be rationally justified. One should carefully distinguish the question of historical genesis from the question of validity. Furthermore, "rational justification" need not entail the idea of resting on a firm ahistorical foundation. Rorty himself makes this very point when he notes that thinkers such as John Dewey, Michael Oakeshott, and John Rawls "have all helped to undermine the idea of a transhistorical 'absolutely valid' set of concepts which would serve as 'philosophical foundations' of liberalism. But each thought of this undermining as a way of strengthening liberal institutions" (Rorty 1989: 57). Each of the three might agree with *this* characterization of their endeavors, but I suspect that they would strongly dissent from what Rorty goes on to say: "All three would happily grant that a *circular justification* of our practices, a justification which makes one feature of our culture look good by citing still another or comparing our culture invidiously with others by reference to our own standards, is the only sort of justification we are going to get" (Rorty 1989: 57, emphasis added). Rorty is not simply claiming that final vocabularies are historical and contingent. Nor is he just asserting the fallibility of all our justifications. Despite his professed skepticism about philosophical theses, he is advancing an extremely *strong* philosophical claim. *No* rational justification of any final vocabulary is possible (not even a fallible justification) *if "rational justification" is taken to mean presenting a non-circular argument to justify or support such a vocabulary.*[13]

Bringing out the radicalness of Rorty's understanding of contingency and irony highlights a worry that has concerned many of his most sympathetic critics (including myself).[14] Suppose we drop the fraught charge of "bad relativism" and ask in a straightforward manner what sorts of considerations would lead us to adopt one final vocabulary rather than another – or even to change our own final vocabularies. (I deliberately use the vague term "considerations" rather than the more fraught term "reasons.") This brings us back to my critique of Rorty's distinction between "argument" and "redescription." Rorty, I suggested, tends to caricature the meaning and role of argument in everyday life as well as in philosophical debates. He makes it seem as if all argument is the sort of thing for which there are clear algorithms by which we can determine their validity. Of course, there *are* such arguments, and many alleged arguments turn out to be invalid on strictly logical grounds. But *living argument*, especially in philosophy, rarely fits this caricature. The rhetorical and polemical force of Rorty's frequent references to "noncircular arguments" or "noncircular theoretical backup" is parasitic upon his caricature of argument. I also argued that there is something disingenuous about the contrast he draws between "argument" and "redescription." Rorty misleads us into thinking that redescription doesn't involve argument. Rorty's redescriptions are shot through with arguments (good and bad arguments). And he certainly seeks to "justify" the positions that he is advocating.

If we abandon Rorty's distinction between "argument" and "redescription," then we can better understand the significance of his approach to irony. I don't think that Rorty is abandoning the idea of justification. Rather, he is opening up the very meaning of justification; he is proposing a new way of thinking about justification. There is a negative and a positive dimension to his proposal. On the negative side, he stands in the tradition of those like Kierkegaard, Nietzsche, and William James who use parody, satire, and irony to mock the very idea of establishing firm "rational justifications" as the central task of philosophy. There have always been philosophers who think that to give up the search for rational justification is to abandon philosophy itself. This is the way in which many of Rorty's severest critics read him. But there is a more positive (and I suggest, *pace* Rorty, "reasonable") way of reading Rorty. He redescribes and *revises* our understanding of justification. Justification in philosophy is never simply a matter of coming up with the best arguments to support our claims. Justification is always addressed to a specific audience. So what counts as justification at one historical time may not be considered an adequate justification at a different historical time. If we are honest, Rorty claims, then we have to recognize that justification involves the use of metaphors, stories, narratives, indirect discourse, redescriptions, imaginative speculations, and humor – indeed, the full range of rhetorical and persuasive devices that are frequently blended together. These are not simply accidental accretions to the justification of final vocabularies; they are *intrinsic* to the activity of justifying. The ironist thinks that those who *pretend* to do more – to do something "purer," "more rigorous," and "more rational" – are *deceiving* themselves.[15]

I am suggesting that we can read ("the reasonable") Rorty as seeking to *exorcise* the picture of vertical, "strict" justification and as urging us to substitute a more adequate conception of horizontal justification. The vertical model is one such that we are never satisfied – never think that something is *really* justified – unless it is grounded on some solid epistemological bedrock. Anything less than this is said to rest on shifting quicksand. The horizontal model is much more complex and messy, but much closer to *living* practices of justification, where we move backward and forward over the web of our beliefs and commitments – modifying, rejecting, and criticizing some of these in light of other beliefs and commitments. One can call this "circular" if one accepts the norms of vertical justification as the only *proper* norm for all justification; but this process is actually more like an enlarged hermeneutical circle rather than the picture of vicious circularity that comes to mind when we tacitly accept the vertical model of justification. Hilary Putnam likes to cite John Austin's dictum, "Enough is enough, enough isn't everything." And this is true for what we count as justification of final vocabularies.[16]

Interpreting Rorty's ironist in this manner can be liberating – liberating from a picture of rational justification that holds many philosophers captive. It also helps to elucidate what it means to play off one vocabulary against another. We seek to justify – in this *horizontal* sense – the final vocabulary that we favor. This activity also involves highlighting its attractive features and exposing the deficiencies of alternatives. And, of course, this type of justification is *always* open to further questioning and revision. From the ironist's perspective, it is only a tempting illusion to think that in philosophy there are (or even that there ought to be) knock-down theoretical arguments or rigorous ahistorical transcendental arguments that are immune from revision.

When Rorty introduces his figure of the "liberal ironist," he shows that irony is *not* a form of complete detachment from worldly affairs. On the contrary, irony is compatible with a *passionate* liberal commitment to diminishing cruelty and humiliation; indeed, it *enables* this commitment. It releases us from the hopeless task of providing a "solid" vertical justification for the liberalism that Rorty advocates and opens the possibility for horizontal justification. Of course, one may raise all sorts of criticisms about Rorty's liberalism. Many readers of Rorty are shocked when he declares: "For liberal ironists, there is no answer to the question 'Why not be cruel?' – no noncircular theoretical backup for the belief that cruelty is horrible" (Rorty 1989: p. xv). But we can give a plausible, positive interpretation of this seemingly outrageous claim. There is no answer to this question *insofar* as it tacitly presupposes the possibility of providing a vertical justification – one that gives solid "theoretical backup." It is also an illusion to think that there are permanent, clear criteria for determining what is cruel. But Rorty's ironist can appeal to other horizontal values and beliefs to support why she takes a particular act or practice to be cruel. In speaking of "horizontal justification," I do not want to suggest that all our values, convictions, and commitments are on the same level – or even that we are fully aware of what they entail. When confronted with a serious moral or political conflict, we may come to realize that some readjustment must be made in our final vocabularies. Encountering unprecedented situations and contingencies may require that we revise or even abandon what we *take* to be final. Rorty's ironist might well adopt Wittgenstein's remark: "Once I have exhausted the justifications, I have reached bedrock, and my spade is turned. Then I am inclined to say 'This is simply what I do'" (Wittgenstein 2014: 91). Giving up on *theoretical* backup is no obstacle to a firm *practical* commitment to diminishing cruelty. The "liberal ironist" knows all too well that there are other possible final vocabularies – including those in which cruelty is redescribed in such a manner as to make it look permissible and even necessary. (Consider the recent "redescription" of torture as "enhanced interrogation.") Because Rorty knows that this is a *real* possibility, he is passionate about his *practical commitment* to his version of liberalism.

Irony, for Rorty, is the means for becoming *re-attached* to worldly projects. In this respect, Rorty is very close in spirit to one of his heroes, Dewey, who also called for philosophers to abandon the problems of philosophy and deal with the problems of human beings.[17] In Rorty's terms, this means giving up the fruitless search for theoretical backup for our political and moral convictions and getting on with concretely fostering the practices of open, tolerant liberalism. This can be achieved only by increasing our sympathetic *solidarity* with our fellow human beings, and not by obsessing about issues of objectivity and truth. Rorty fits within, and contributes novel insights to, the tradition of relating irony to living a human (and humane) life.

Despite what, at times, may seem to be striking differences, Rorty can be seen as also belonging within a tradition exemplified by Socrates and Kierkegaard. Rorty's Socrates is an ironist who shows us that one can live a virtuous life without theoretical backup. Knowing *how* to live one's life does not require vertical rational justification. According to Rorty, it is Plato, not Socrates, who initiates the search for firm rational foundations. Rorty's Kierkegaard is an ironist who is a master at undermining the pretentions and illusions of Philosophy with a capital "P." Although Rorty would back way from any essentialist claims about irony or human life, he certainly would affirm that irony can liberate us from deeply misleading illusions and can help enable us to live more humane lives with our fellow human creatures.

Finally, I want to return to Kierkegaard, the thinker who initiated Lear's case for irony. Although, as Vlastos points out, it was Cicero and Quintilian who canonized Socrates as the supreme ironist, we must remember that the use of the term *eirōneia* (and its cognates) appears very infrequently in Plato's dialogues. Only with Schlegel and the Romantics does Socratic irony move to the very foreground of the interpretation of the Platonic dialogues. Kierkegaard's early investigation of irony stands in the shadow of Schlegel's radical interpretation of Romantic irony and the sharp critiques that it provoked – especially by Hegel and the Hegelians.[18] Keeping in mind this background of the Romantics and Hegel's critique of the Romantics is essential for understanding the structure of *The Concept of Irony*. Both Hegel and Kierkegaard reject what they take to be the self-defeating excesses of Romantic irony. In the first (and longest) part of *The Concept of Irony*, Kierkegaard engages in a detailed reinterpretation of the *Apology*, *Symposium*, *Protagoras*, *Phaedo*, *Gorgias*, and Book I of the *Republic*. In each case, he draws out what these dialogues contribute to our understanding of Socratic irony. His interpretations are always provocative, even if at times they are idiosyncratic. They are what Richard Rorty (following Harold Bloom) calls "strong readings." Much of the fascinating detail of his interpretations gets lost when Kierkegaard characterizes Socratic irony as "infinite absolute negativity."

Despite Magister Kierkegaard's swerve away from Hegel in his dissertation, his pseudonymous author Johannes Climacus revises this early understanding of irony. However, there are several features of Kierkegaard's initial discussion of irony that he never repudiated. And they are important for understanding irony – how it is both destructive and liberating. Magister Kierkegaard's portrait of Socrates as epitomizing nihilistic negativity is exaggerated and distortive, but, nevertheless, this portrayal enables Kierkegaard to highlight the radical *disruptive* questioning that Socratic irony initiates. In this respect, I think Lear is right when (inspired by Kierkegaard) he stresses that the uncanny experience of irony must be sufficiently disruptive and disorienting to bring about right-hand radical questioning. For Kierkegaard, this is an *essential* condition for achieving the *beginning* of subjectivity and inwardness. Kierkegaard knows that there is an enormous temptation (as illustrated by the Sophists and some of his contemporaries) to *pretend* to engage in radical questioning when one is actually smuggling in unexamined prejudices. Kierkegaard knows what it takes to overcome this self-deception and to give up deeply held illusions. This radical "nihilistic" questioning can be terrifying, dangerous, and liberating: *terrifying* because it means giving up the familiar banisters and guidelines that we normally accept in orienting our lives; *dangerous* because, when such questioning is truly radical, it seems to leave us with nothing; *liberating* because it frees us from illusions and enables us to confront our subjectivity and inwardness without illusions.

This way of characterizing irony is very close to the way in which Hannah Arendt describes *thinking*. To exemplify what she means by thinking (which she sharply distinguishes from knowledge), she too appeals to Socrates.[19] Her depiction of Socrates as a thinker complements what Kierkegaard says about Socrates as an ironist. Arendt comments on the similes that Socrates used to characterize himself, as well as the simile used by others to characterize him: gadfly, midwife, and electric ray. "*First*, Socrates is a gadfly: he knows how to arouse the citizens who, without him will 'sleep on undisturbed for the rest of their lives', unless someone comes along to wake them up again" (Arendt 1971: 432). *Second*, Socrates is a midwife. And the irony here is that "looking at the Socratic dialogues there is nobody among Socrates' interlocutors who ever brought forth a thought that was no wind egg. He rather did what Plato, certainly thinking of Socrates, said about the sophists; he purged people of their 'opinions'...*Third*, Socrates knowing that we don't know and still unwilling to let it go at that, remains steadfast with his own perplexities and like the electric ray, paralyzes with them whomever he comes into contact with" (Arendt 1971: 432–3).[20] It isn't that Socrates, knowing the answers to the questions that he raises, seeks to perplex other people. Rather, he infects them with the perplexities that he himself deeply experiences. Kierkegaard would agree with this three-fold characterization of Socrates. But the parallel between Arendt and Kierkegaard goes deeper. What she says about thinking is precisely what Kierkegaard says about Socrates' irony. "[T]hinking inevitably has a destructive, undermining effect on all established criteria, values of conduct we treat in morals and ethics" (Arendt 1971: 435). As Kierkegaard makes clear in the second part of *The Concept of Irony*, if we *reify* this infinite absolute negativity of irony – if we never move beyond it, we will find ourselves in the self-destructive paradoxes of the Romantic ironists. Or as Johannes Climacus tells us in the *Post-script*, Magister Kierkegaard brought out one aspect only of irony – and thereby distorts the meaning of irony. Again, Arendt makes a point that nicely complements Kierkegaard's mature understanding of irony.

> What we commonly call nihilism – and are tempted to date historically, decry politically, and ascribe to thinkers who allegedly dared to think "dangerous thoughts" – is actually a danger inherent in the thinking activity itself. There are no dangerous thoughts, *thinking itself is dangerous, but nihilism is not its product.* Nihilism is but the other side of conventionalism; its creed consists in negations of the current, so-called positive values to which it remains bound. All critical examination must go through a stage of at least hypothetically negating accepted opinions and "values" by finding out their implications and tacit assumptions, and in this sense nihilism may be seen as an ever-present danger of thinking. But this danger doesn't arise out of the Socratic conviction that an unexamined life is not worth living but, on the contrary, out of a desire to find results which would make further thinking unnecessary. Thinking is equally dangerous to all creeds and, by itself, does not bring forth any new creed. (Arendt 1971: 435, emphasis added)

What are the lessons that we learn from *The Concept of Irony* – lessons that Kierkegaard never gave up – and which are vital for understanding how irony is related to living a human life? (1) Irony as epitomized by Socrates demands radical questioning of all conventional understandings of morality. The ironist lives without being seduced by illusions and self-delusions. (2) This radical disruptive questioning is a necessary moment in facing up to one's subjectivity and inwardness. (3) If this negative attitude remains frozen and reified, if the ironist never gets beyond this destructive activity, then the ironist project is self-defeating. (4) Although the final pages of *The Concept of Irony* gesture toward a way out from this dead end, Kierkegaard fails to show us how we can move to what he calls "the truth of irony."

In *Concluding Unscientific Postscript*, Johannes Climacus emphasizes what is missing from Magister Kierkegaard's conception of irony: "the unity of ethical passion." Lear helps to illuminate the thrust of Kierkegaard's (and Climacus's) point. Unlike an ordinary experience of uncanny disruption – where we may remain frozen – the genuine experience of irony involves "a passion for a certain direction." This directed passion is exemplified in Socrates' *Eros*, Socrates doesn't simply manifest *Eros*; he incarnates *Eros* that shapes his entire life. We, as "single individuals," must try to do *for ourselves* what Socrates does. This is what I take Kierkegaard to mean by the "truth of irony." All the devices that he employs – indirect communication, irony, satire, parody, creating different pseudonymous authors – are used to get *us* – his readers (and perhaps himself) – to *personally* experience erotic passion that is manifested in existential choices. And Kierkegaard knows that, at best, he can only lead us to this experience of irony. Nothing that he, or anyone else, can say or write can compel us to make these inward choices and decisions. No one can provide arguments that are sufficient to tell us how to live our lives. There is always a *gap* between what can be *said* by philosophers and what we as individuals actually choose. This gap is where our individual *freedom* manifests itself. Exercising this inward passionate freedom is what it means to live a human life. This is why to become human does not come that easily.[21]

Why Irony Matters

I began this study by quoting the opening remarks of D. C. Muecke's *The Compass of Irony*, where he compares getting a grip on irony with trying to gather the nebulous mist. Even Wayne Booth begins his famous *A Rhetoric of Irony* by warning his readers that "once a term [irony] has been used to cover just about everything there is, it perhaps ought simply to be retired" (Booth 1974: p. ix). Despite the popularity of various approaches to irony by literary critics, rhetoricians, and media theorists, irony has not been a prominent topic in contemporary philosophy. This may seem odd, because virtually all discussions of irony – from almost any perspective – take us back to Socratic irony. One common virtue of Lear, Rorty, Vlastos, and Nehamas is that they are attuned to the philosophical significance of irony. I believe that one of the reasons for this recent interest in a philosophical investigation of irony is to redress an imbalance of contemporary professional academic philosophy.

Academic philosophy today has become almost exclusively what Nehamas calls a theoretical discipline – a discipline in which the theses that one advances and the arguments used to justify these claims are all-important, a discipline that has little to do with the ways in which we each live our lives. I have no desire to denigrate or ridicule the profession to which I belong. Nor do I think it helpful to engage in nostalgia for an "idealized" past that is frequently little more than a product of one's imagination. But I do think that there is something worrying about the growing academic professionalization of philosophy and the way we train students in philosophy. In a wonderful essay, "The Rhythm of Education," A. N. Whitehead describes the rhythm of education as consisting of three stages: romance, precision, and generalization. "The stage of romance is the stage of first apprehension. The subject-matter has the vividness of novelty; it holds within itself unexplored connexions with possibilities half-disclosed by glimpses and half-concealed by the wealth of material" (Whitehead 1929: 17). What Whitehead calls "romance" is close to how Diotima describes *Eros* in the *Symposium* – and is embodied by Socrates as the passionate lover of wisdom. Many (perhaps most) students who are attracted to the study of philosophy initially experience something like this erotic romance. But romance is the first stage only in the rhythm of education. Romance needs to be followed by a second stage, which Whitehead calls "precision." "In this stage, width of relationship is subordinated to exactness of formulation" (Whitehead 1929: 18). Romance without precision is in danger of becoming sentimental. *Eros* needs to be channeled and directed. But precision without romance is in danger of becoming mere *pedantry*. "It is evident," Whitehead declares, "that a stage of precision is barren without a previous stage of romance; unless there are facts which have already been vaguely apprehended in their broad generality, the previous analysis is an analysis of nothing. It is simply a series of meaningless statements about bare facts, produced artificially and without further relevance" (Whitehead 1929: 18). The final stage in this rhythm, generalization, "is a return to romanticism with the added advantage of classified ideas and relevant technique. It is the fruition which has been the goal of precise training" (Whitehead 1929: 19). Whitehead compares this stage with "Hegel's synthesis." This rhythm of romance–precision–generalization is one that is (or rather, ought to be) iterated throughout one's life. "Education should consist in a continual repetition of such cycles" (Whitehead 1929: 19). Whitehead – who declared that the European philosophical tradition consists of a series of footnotes to Plato – is reformulating a view of education that was anticipated by Plato.

Using Whitehead's schema, I worry that academic philosophy today is doing everything it can to kill the romantic erotic impulse in our students. We have become so obsessed with precision that we lose sight of its goal. Philosophy as an academic discipline is in danger of becoming barren, pedantic, and irrelevant.[22] This is why I think that the turn to a philosophical investigation of irony as it relates to living a human life is so important and relevant today. I have sought to bring out the strengths and weaknesses of the contributions of Lear, Rorty, Vlastos, and Nehamas. I have not hesitated to criticize them where I think they go wrong. Nor have I attempted to diminish their sharp disagreements with each other. Nevertheless, each contributes something vital to a richer and deeper understanding of how irony can shape the way in which we live our lives in a community – in the polis. They enable us to return with fresh insight to those two great ironists, Kierkegaard and Socrates. They help us to appreciate anew the subtle dialectic between philosophy as a theoretical discipline and philosophy as the art of living. They all remind us of Socrates' bold and provocative declaration in *Republic* 1: 352d – one that has, and continues to, reverberate throughout the ages: "It is not *any* question we are dealing with, but rather *how should one live?*"

Notes

Chapter 1   Jonathan Lear and Richard Rorty on Irony

1   In addition to Lear's two lectures, this volume includes commentaries by Christine M. Korsgaard, Richard Moran, Cora Diamond, and Robert A. Paul. Lear responds to each of these commentaries. I will be focusing on Lear's first lecture, where he explains what he means by the experience of irony, the capacity for irony, and ironic existence.

2   This is also the title of Lear's first lecture. Lear explains why he begins his examination with a single journal entry rather than a historical or critical survey of the various interpretations of irony. See Lear 2011: 180 n. 12. In this same note he also provides a list of sources that deal with various aspects of irony.

3   Lear makes it clear that there are nonverbal ways that can be part of social pretense: e.g., the way I dress, my mannerisms, my sense of pride and shame can express my social pretense as a professor. They are all ways of putting oneself forward *as* a professor.

4   It should be clear from the example of Christendom that there is a historicity to practical identities. Some practical identities (and social roles) are relatively constant (like being a parent), but some come into being and pass away. Lear stresses this point in his book *Radical Hope*, where he discusses Plenty Coups, the last Indian chief of the American Crow Indian tribe. The possibility of fulfilling the aspiration of being a Crow *warrior* made sense among the Crow in 1850. By 1890, however, when the tribe was ensconced on a reservation and intertribal warfare was forbidden, the pretense and aspiration of being a Crow *warrior* disappeared; it no longer made any sense. Lear also argues that even after it was no longer possible to have the practical identity of a Crow

warrior, Plenty Coups did manifest the virtue of courage. (See Lear 2006: 44)

5   Although Lear dramatizes the moment of ironic uncanny disruption to highlight its distinctiveness, he tells us that there are also "petite moments of ironic uncanniness that are almost over as soon as they begin. These moments happen to us, we get over them quickly and move on, remembering at best a shadow of their occurrence" (Lear 2011: 21).

6   According to Lear, the answer to each of these questions is not the formulation of a new set of criteria for characterizing *the* politician, *the* rhetorician, or *the* wise person. Rather, Plato's answer to these questions is: There is Socrates, for he is the one who understands the real political craft, exemplifies the excellence of the true rhetorician and the wisdom of the one who knows that he does not know.

7   Cora Diamond questions Lear's thesis about the concepts by means of which we understand ourselves. See her commentary and Lear's response in Lear 2011: 128–63.

8   "One might have thought that since ironic experience is uncanny disruption, we must be passive sufferers. Indeed, in the first instance we are; but it is possible to become active with respect to one's own ironic experience" (Lear 2011: 42).

9   In the second appendix, Lear criticizes James Conant's thesis that "all the confusions that Kierkegaard's method brings to light are ultimately grammatical (in Wittgenstein's sense of the term)" (Lear 2011: 41).

10   Lear says that "his point here is not to criticize Rorty"; but this strikes me as disingenuous because, according to Lear, if there are no "right-hand resonances," then there really is no ironic experience. And in his response to Richard Moran, Lear accuses Rorty of leaving irony out of his account – that is, leaving out *what Lear claims irony really is* (see Lear 2011: 119–20).

11   Bjørn Ramberg also discusses some of the relations between Lear and Rorty on irony. Ramberg is especially concerned with emphasizing the political relevance of Rorty's notion of the "liberal ironist." See Ramberg 2015.

12   I am thinking of the experiences that led up to Rorty's decision to leave the Princeton philosophy department and to accept a position as a professor of humanities at the University of Virginia. For Rorty's discussion of these events see Rorty 1999a. See also Bernstein 2010: 200–16.

13   See Bernstein 2010: 200–16, where I discuss this transformation.

14   Consider how well Lear's description of the experience of irony fits Rorty's experience. "When irony hits its mark, the person who is its target has an uncanny experience that the demands of an ideal, value, or identity to which he takes himself to be already committed dramatically transcend the received social understandings" (Lear 2011: 25).

15   Even in some of his early "analytic" articles one can detect Rorty's use of irony: e.g., when Rorty elaborated a version of "eliminative materialism," he was not primarily *advocating* it as a substantive doctrine, but rather engaging in an imaginative thought experiment to call into question the popular view at the time: namely, that the task of philosophy is to engage in conceptual analysis. On such a view of philosophy, it would be a category mistake – a conceptual confusion – to claim that the mind is identical with the brain.

16   See my critique of Rorty's interpretation of Dewey in Bernstein 1986: 21–57.

17   In his "Intellectual Autobiography" Rorty writes:

> Although I had begun to read the later Heidegger in the course of the 1970s and had become convinced of his importance and of Derrida's, I had not, at the time I was finishing the *Mirror*, been able to tell myself a coherent story about the relation between postpositivistic analytic philosophy, American pragmatism, and Heidegger's "history of Being." The essays I wrote in the 1980s ... were attempts to piece together such a story. I came to think that the critical turning point in modern philosophy was Hegel's off-hand, yet pregnant, claim that philosophy is "its time held in thought." So in those pieces I dropped the awkward "systematic" versus "edifying" distinction I had drawn in *Mirror*, and instead simply opposed bad ahistoricist to good historicist philosophizing. (Auxier and Hahn 2010: 13–14)

Although Rorty dropped the systematic/edifying distinction, he never repudiated the importance of satire, parody, and irony in historicist philosophizing.

18   In his discussion of the difference between systematic and edifying philosophizing, Rorty has an intriguing footnote: "The permanent fascination of the man who dreamed up the whole idea of Western philosophy – Plato – is that we still do not know which sort of philosopher he was. Even if the *Seventh Letter* is set aside as spurious, the fact that after millenniums of commentary nobody knows which passages in the dialogues are jokes keeps the puzzle fresh" (Rorty 1979: 369). Compare this with what Goethe wrote: "He who would explain to us when men like Plato spoke in earnest, when in jest or half-jest, what they wrote from conviction and what merely for the sake of the argument, would certainly render us an extraordinary service and contribute greatly to our education" (quoted in Nehamas 1998: 7).

19   See my discussion of Rorty's critique of the philosophical appeal to intuitions in Bernstein 2014.

20   For an illuminating discussion of the meaning and centrality of Rorty's notion of a vocabulary, see Robert Brandom's "Vocabularies of Pragmatism: Synthesizing Naturalism and Historicism" and Rorty's response in Brandom 2000: 156–90. Rorty concedes that his notion of a

vocabulary is fuzzy (there are no clear criteria for distinguishing one vocabulary from another). Nevertheless, he maintains that "it is vocabularies all the way down." He also writes: "I have no criterion of individuation for distinct languages or vocabularies to offer, but I am not sure we need one" (Rorty 1989: 7, n. 1).

21   In *Beyond Good and Evil*, Nietzsche declares: "With stiff seriousness that inspires laughter, all our philosophers demanded something far more exalted, presumptuous, and solemn from themselves as soon as they approached the study of morality; they wanted to supply a rational foundation for morality – and every philosopher so far has believed that he has provided such a foundation" (Nietzsche 1989: 9).

22   In response to a sympathetic, but penetrating, critique by J. B. Schneewind concerning the "radical doubts" of the ironist, Rorty concedes that his description of the liberal ironist was "badly flawed."

> I conflated two quite different sorts of people: the unruffled pragmatist and the anguished existentialist adolescent. I make it sound as if you could not be an antifoundationalist and romantic self-creator without becoming a Sartrean, ever conscious of the abyss. But one can be both and remain, as far as philosophy goes, a placid Deweyan – someone who is a nominalist and an historicist, but not much troubled by doubt either about philosophical doctrine or about her own moral or political outlook. It was a mistake to suggest (as I did on p. 87 of *Contingency, Irony, and Solidarity*) that all ironist intellectuals were afflicted with such doubts. (Auxier and Hahn 2010: 506)

I agree with Schneewind and Ramberg that Rorty's emphasis on "radical doubts" is misleading insofar as it appears that Rorty can be misinterpreted as an epistemological skeptic. (See Schneewind 2010 and Ramberg 2015.) Rorty's point is existential *in the sense* that the ironist is aware of the plurality of final vocabularies, and that there is no standpoint outside and above these vocabularies from which to evaluate them. This is why redescription (not argument) plays such an important role in creating new vocabularies.

23   Rorty anticipates this point when he draws a sharp contrast between epistemology and hermeneutics in *Philosophy and the Mirror of Nature*. "Epistemology," Rorty tells us, is the

> desire to find 'foundations' to which one might cling, frameworks beyond which one must not stray, objects which impose themselves, representations which cannot be gainsaid... In the interpretation I shall be offering, 'hermeneutics' is not the name for a discipline, nor for a method of achieving the sort of results which epistemology failed to achieve, nor a program of research. On the contrary, hermeneutics is an expression of the hope that the cultural space left open by the demise of epistemology will not be filled – that our culture should become one in which the demand for constraint and confrontation is no longer felt. (Rorty 1979: 315)

24   See the exchange between Putnam and Rorty (Putnam 1990 and Rorty 1993). See also my discussion of Rorty's "relativism" in Bernstein 1986: 40–2.

25   See my criticisms of this claim about redescription in Bernstein 1991: 277–82.

26   "Blind impress" refers to a poem by Philip Larkin (see Rorty 1989: 23).

27   Lear is emphatic that Freud (like Plato) shows that the soul has a structure: "Psychoanalysis commends itself to our attention because it takes seriously the idea that the soul has a structure. Indeed, [psychoanalysis] is a peculiar form of conversation that aims to bring about a structural change in the soul" (Lear 2005: 443).

28   Despite the sharp differences between Lear and Rorty, there is an intriguing convergence in their broad understanding of the meaning and significance of poetry. In *Radical Hope*, when speaking about the possibility of a new Crow poet who could take up the Crow past and "project it into vibrant new ways for the Crow to live and to be," Lear writes: "Here by 'poet' I mean the broadest sense of a creative maker of meaningful space. The possibility for such a poet is precisely the possibility for the creation of a new field of possibilities" (Lear 2006: 51). Compare this with Rorty's characterization of the poet in *Contingency, Irony, and Solidarity*.
   Rorty draws upon Harold Bloom's conception of the "strong poet" as someone who creates something that is genuinely new – someone who thereby creates new possibilities. So Rorty, like Lear, is using "poet" in a broad sense. "I assume that Bloom would be willing to extend the reference to 'poet' beyond those who write in verse, and to use it in the large, generic sense in which I am using it – so that Proust and Nabokov, Newton and Darwin, Hegel and Heidegger, also fall under the term" (Rorty 1989: 24, n. 1). Furthermore, there is also an intriguing correspondence in their conceptions of hope. Rorty would certainly agree with Lear when he declares: "Radical hope anticipates a good for which those who have the hope as yet lack the appropriate concepts with which to understand it" (Lear 2006: 103). This corresponds to what Rorty calls "ungroundable hope." Rorty's last collection of articles is *Philosophy and Social Hope* (1999).

29   Quoted in Vlastos 1991: 28.

30   Of course, "self-understanding" presupposes linguistic ability, but the *experience* of irony – the uncanny ironic disruption – need not be expressed in language. For Lear, the experience of irony is not a figure of speech (or writing).

31   Lear uses the translation of the *Symposium* by Thomas Griffith.

32   Compare Lear's interpretation of Socrates' silence with Nehamas's observation: "We shall never know what occupied Socrates during his habitual and often long periods of silence. They must have baffled Plato himself, since he never tries to explain them: they are simply part of

what Socrates was…Socrates' silence may have been either interruptions or essential elements of his communicative endeavor: we shall never know" (Nehamas 1998: 84).

33   Compare Lear's and Korsgaard's interpretation of Socrates' behavior at Potidaea with Hegel's interpretation in his *Lectures on the History of Philosophy*.

> In this campaign [Potidaea] it is said that once, sunk in deep meditation, he stood immovable on one spot the whole day and night, until the morning sun awoke him from his trance – a condition in which he is said often to have been. This was a cataleptic state, which may bear some relation to magnetic somnambulism, in which Socrates became quite dead to sensuous consciousness. From this physical setting free of the inward abstract self from the concrete bodily existence of the individual, we have, in the outward manifestation, a proof of how the depths of his mind worked within him. (Hegel 1968: 390–1)

Whatever else Lear might say about this interpretation, I scarcely think he would describe it as "flatfooted."

34   There is another awkward consequence of Lear's understanding of irony. Lear tell us: "When irony hits its mark, the person who is the target has an uncanny experience that the demands of an ideal, value, or identity to which he takes himself to be already committed dramatically transcend the received social understandings" (Lear 2011: 25). But is there textual evidence that *any* of Socrates' interlocutors have this sort of "uncanny experience"? Does this mean that Socrates' irony never "hits its mark"?

35   Although Lear speaks here of Socrates' way of teaching virtue, in an earlier article he tells us that "if one looks at the dialogues in which the *elenchus* is used [the so-called early dialogues], there is no evidence that any interlocutors are improved by the conversation. Indeed, they often seem irritated, fed up, anxious to leave" (Lear 2005: 442).

36   In *Radical Hope*, Lear speaks of the social role of being a Crow warrior and suggests that one could ask the ironic question: "Among the warriors is there a warrior?" (Lear 2006: 44). Being an *excellent* warrior means killing as many enemies as possible in a courageous and honorable manner by a ritual known as "planting of a coup-stick and counting coups" (Lear 2006: 13).

37   Alasdair MacIntyre raises a related objection in his exchange with Lear. Macintyre, using Lear's example of a teacher, argues that the virtues (excellences) of truthfulness and humility can be achieved without irony. It is because and insofar as irony serves the ends of the virtues of truthfulness and humility that we need it. In his response, Lear concedes that significant ethical improvement can take place without irony. Nevertheless, he still wants to argue that something "ethically significant" is missing in a world without irony. To explain what he means, he

now introduces a distinction between different types of human account-ability. There are some normative dimensions of human life that can be understood as social constructions. Lear's example is the game of baseball, where we can have debates about what makes for a good player. He wants to distinguish social constructions from the subjective category of being a teacher. He tells us: "The subjective category *teacher*, unlike the social role of baseball player, is subject to a normative pull of goodness that outstrips any social construction of what goodness consists in. Here we have a different kind of responsibility for and responsiveness to the goodness of teaching – one which is enigmatic and which can be very unsettling." But teaching, as we well know from historical examples such as Nazi Germany and fanatical religious socie-ties, is not necessarily subject to "the normative pull of goodness." Furthermore, Lear does not really explain how we are to distinguish those practical identities that are "social constructions" from those which are not. And he doesn't clarify what he means by "a different kind of responsibility." Consequently, I don't see how Lear's remarks help to distinguish human excellence from an excellence that is inter-nal to a particular practical identity. (For the exchange between Lear and MacIntyre, see Lear and MacIntyre 2012).

38　In Lear's response to Richard Moran, he writes: "In the lectures, I distinguish *the experience of irony* from *the capacity for irony* and from *ironic existence*. It is only ironic existence that is a human virtue: it is a capacity for putting irony to excellent use in the living of a distinctively human life. Kierkegaard thought it occurred rarely, he took Socrates and himself to be exemplars" (Lear 2011: 119). But what precisely is "putting irony to excellent use"? And why can't one live a distinctively human life even if one does *not* put irony to excellent use?

39　Perhaps Lear's talk about grasping what irony "really is" is itself meant ironically – an indirect way of telling us how *he* thinks we *ought to* think about irony.

40　"For a metaphysician, 'philosophy,' as defined by reference to the canon-ical Plato–Kant sequence, is an attempt to know about certain things – quite general and important things…The metaphysician thinks that although we may not have all the answers, we have already got criteria for the right answers. So he thinks 'right' does not merely mean 'suit-able for those who speak as we do' but has a stronger sense – the sense of 'grasping real essence'" (Rorty 1989: 76).

41　See the exchange between Schneewind and Rorty in Auxier and Hahn 2010: 479–508.

42　There is a fluctuation in Rorty's use of "irony" and "ironist." Although he states that: "Irony seems inherently a private matter" (Rorty 1989: 87), sometimes he has a tendency to use "irony" as a civic virtue that will be exhibited by all citizens in his liberal utopia. They are good liberals who no longer feel the need to "justify" their liberalism or to ask the question "Why not be cruel?" But at other times, Rorty seems to restrict the label "ironist" to philosophers and intellectuals who no longer feel the need to philosophize in a style that calls for rational justification of their final vocabularies. For example, he writes: "In the ideal liberal society, the intellectuals would be ironists, although non-intellectuals would not. The latter would, however, be commonsensically nominalist and historicist. So they would see themselves as contingent through and through, without feeling any particular doubts about the contingencies they happen to be" (Rorty 1989: 87).

43   See Bernstein 1991: 258–92.

44   At times, the "outrageous" Rorty sounds as if he is guilty of what Karl Popper once called "the myth of the framework," where vocabularies are understood to be frameworks that are completely incommensurable with each other. But the "reasonable Rorty" proposes a more moderate position. Although he denies that there are ahistorical standards for evaluating competing vocabularies, he concedes that there is a "dialectical relationship" in adopting new vocabularies and paradigms. For example, in a footnote to his response to Habermas's "Richard Rorty's Pragmatic Turn," he writes: "I entirely agree with Habermas when he says that philosophical 'paradigms do not form an arbitrary sequence but a dialectical relationship.' I regret having given him the impression that I believe that the Way of Things, Ideas and Words are incommensurable with one another. I think of them as having succeeded one another as a result of the need for a Kuhnian 'revolution' in order to overcome piled-up anomalies" (Brandom 2000: 63). But, if this is the way in which Rorty understands the "dialectical relationship" of paradigms and vocabularies, then we can give *reasons*, and not simply *causes*, for why a vocabulary replaces a former one (it overcomes "piled-up anomalies"). To speak of reasons here does not require or presuppose that there is some ahistorical universal standard for evaluating reasons.

45   See e.g. his exchange with Bjørn Ramberg in Brandom 2000: 351–77.

46   In *this respect* there is a similarity not only with Nietzsche and Kierkegaard but also with Wittgenstein (early and late), who claimed that philosophy is essentially an *activity* (not a doctrine) – an activity that exposes philosophical illusions.

47   Given Rorty's passionate concern for, and commitment to, diminishing cruelty and humiliation, Lear's critique of Rorty is not only superficial, but perverse. Consider the following comment by Lear about Rorty:

> If we can only be ironists, our philosophical problems will be over. Instead, we can spend our time in "philosophy" as aesthetic discernment: making fine discriminations among positions, working out the arguments, enjoying the brilliance, laughing at the stupidity – all without risking the instability of commitment. Calling this ideal of detachment "irony" keeps from view the thought that anything is missing – the thought that there

is a phenomenon that is getting left out of account, namely, irony. (Lear 2011: 120)

Lear ascribes to Rorty what Rorty clearly *rejects*. Rorty thinks that most academic philosophers (especially those working in the analytic tradition) subscribe to this "ideal" of detachment. If there is one thing that Rorty hopes will end, it is "making fine discriminations among positions, working out the arguments, enjoying the brilliance, laughing at the stupidity" of those who are not playing the same game. It is this *illusion* of "detachment" in philosophy that Rorty seeks to undermine with his appeal to irony. Furthermore, Lear pays no attention to *why* Rorty introduces the figure of the "liberal ironist." Rorty defends the figure of the "liberal ironist" in order to challenge the ideal of philosophical detachment and to show that one can be *passionately committed* to eliminating (or at least diminishing) cruelty and humiliation and, *at the same time*, accept the contingency of one's central beliefs and desires.

Chapter 2   What is Socratic Irony?

1   e.g., Hegel writes: "But Socrates did not grow like a mushroom out of the earth, for he stands in continuity with his time, and thus is not only a most important figure in the history of Philosophy – perhaps the most interesting in the philosophy of antiquity – but is also a world-famed personage" (Hegel 1968: 384).

2   Vlastos characterizes the "Socratic problem," the problem of establishing whether the Socrates portrayed in the Platonic dialogues is the real historical Socrates or a Platonic fiction, as "the bugbear of Platonic studies."

> The question "Who are you talking about – Socrates *or* a 'Socrates' in Plato?" will dog your steps, barking at you, forcing you to turn and face it in self-defense. If you do mean the former, you must argue for it. You must give reasons for the claim that through a "Socrates" in Plato we can come to know the Socrates of history – the Socrates who made history, taught Plato and others, changed their thinking and their lives, and through them changed the course of Western thought. (Vlastos 1991: 45)

3   The reason why I place "early," "middle," and "late" in scare quotes is because classical scholars are still arguing about which dialogues belong in which group, as well as the basis for dating the dialogues – and even whether this chronological ordering is a helpful way of approaching the Platonic dialogues. For Vlastos's classification of the three chronological groups of dialogues see Vlastos 1991: 46–7. Nehamas's grouping is similar to Vlastos's. But, unlike Vlastos, Nehamas considers the *Gorgias* to be a middle dialogue, not an early dialogue. See Nehamas 1998: 196,

n. 33. These differing classifications have important consequences for how Vlastos and Nehamas interpret Socratic irony. Charles Kahn provides a helpful overview of the controversial procedures that classical scholars employ in order to develop their chronological ordering of the dialogues. See Kahn 1996: 42–8.

4 For the listing of these ten theses see Vlastos 1991: 47–9.

5 The following is Vlastos's listing of his first four theses:

IA. $Socrates_E$ is exclusively a moral philosopher.

IB. $Socrates_M$ is a moral philosopher *and* metaphysician *and* epistemologist *and* philosopher of science *and* philosopher of language *and* philosopher of religion *and* philosopher of education *and* philosopher of art. The whole encyclopedia of philosophical science is his domain.

IIB. $Socrates_M$ had a grandiose metaphysical theory of "separately existing" Forms and of a separable soul which learns by "recollecting" pieces of its pre-natal fund of knowledge.

IIA. $Socrates_E$ has no such theory.

IIIA. $Socrates_E$, seeking knowledge elenctically, keeps avowing that he has none.

IIIB. $Socrates_M$ seeks demonstrative knowledge and is confident that he finds it.

IVB. $Socrates_M$ has a complex, tripartite model of the soul.

IVA. $Socrates_E$ knows nothing of this model, which would have unsettled his conception of moral virtue and undercut his doctrine of the impossibility of incontinence (*akrasia*). (Vlastos 1991: 47–8)

"The most we could learn from his [Plato's] writings is that in different periods in his life he puts into the mouth of Socrates philosophies which are not only different, but, in important respects, antithetical" (Vlastos 1991: 81). But Vlastos wants to show that in the early dialogues we "can come to know the thought of Socrates of history" (Vlastos 1991: 81). In chapter 3, entitled "The Evidence of Aristotle and Xenophon," he argues that we find in their descriptions of Socrates *independent* evidence to support the claim that $Socrates_E$ in Plato's dialogues is an accurate representation of the historical Socrates.

6 There is a long tradition in Plato studies of stressing the unity (rather than the development) of Plato's thought. John M. Cooper presents a strong case for *not* making chronological assumptions about the writing of the Platonic dialogues in his Introduction to Plato (Plato 1997). See also Nehamas's discussion of the issue of chronology in Nehamas 1998: 219, n. 64.

7 In speaking of the dialogue as a fictional form, Kahn does *not* mean that Socrates (and the other interlocutors of the dialogues) are fictional in the way in which Hamlet or King Lear are fictional characters created by Shakespeare. They are not pure creative inventions. Rather, his point

is that some of Plato's characters (including Socrates) are *imaginative* recreations of real persons. He also contests the evidence from external sources such as Aristotle and Xenophon for establishing what the historical Socrates was like. Kahn does think that, on the basis of the early Platonic dialogues, especially the *Apology*, we can develop a "minimal view" of the historical Socrates. "As the literary version of a public speech, composed not by the speaker but by a member of the audience, the *Apology* can properly be regarded as a quasi-historical document like Thucydides' version of Pericles' Funeral Oration" (Kahn 1996: 88). For Kahn's general discussion of maximal and minimal views of Socrates (based on Plato's dialogues) see Kahn 1996: 73–95. For another approach to the problem of fiction and Socrates see Sarah Kofman, *Socrates: Fictions of a Philosopher*. She writes: "With Socrates, we cannot escape from fiction" (Kofman 1998: 1).

8   See Vlastos 1991: 23–4 for the evidence to support this claim.

9   The *eirōn* is a typical character in Ancient Greek New Comedy. He is not portrayed as a willful deceiver. He can appear as intentionally humble, under-appreciating himself (*eirōn*) or as intentionally boastful, over-appreciating himself (*alazon*).

10   Neither of these two senses of "pretend" matches perfectly Lear's use of "pretense."

11   I don't think it is accidental that Vlastos uses this Wittgensteinian expression. He is claiming that this new *form of life* involves a new form of meaning of *eirōneia*. The expression "form of life" (*Lebensform*) appears only three times in Wittgenstein's *Philosophical Investigations* (paragraphs 19, 23, and 241), yet the expression has taken on a life of its own. In paragraph 23, he writes: "The word 'language-*game*' is used here to emphasize the fact that the speaking of language is part of an activity, or form of life" (Wittgenstein 2014: 15). The expression, "form of life," when applied to Socrates, is intended to highlight how what Socrates *says* and *does* (his activity) form an integral and distinctive *unity*.

12   Vlastos concludes his chapter on Socratic irony with a caveat. He tells us that in the course of his inquiry he stumbled on something that he had not reckoned on at the start. "In that small segment of evidence I have scrutinized we can see how Socrates could have deceived without intending to deceive. If you are a young Alcibiades courted by Socrates you are left to your own devices to decide what to make of his riddling ironies. If you go wrong and he sees that you have gone wrong, he may not lift a finger to dispel your error, far less feel the obligation to knock it out of your head" (Vlastos 1991: 44). Nevertheless, this caveat about the possibility of *unintentional* deception does not detract from his main claim that the irony does not involve *willful* deception.

13   Strictly speaking, "the great philosophical paradoxes" in the early Platonic dialogue turn out, on Vlastos's analysis, not to be genuine paradoxes. Once we grasp that there are *different* senses of "knowing" and

"teaching" in Socrates' use of complex irony, we realize that Socrates' disavowals of knowing and teaching are not really paradoxical, because the sense in which Socrates disavows knowledge is not the same as the sense in which he does have knowledge. And the same is true with teaching. Socrates doesn't teach by transferring knowledge to the learner's mind; but he does teach insofar as he engages his interlocutors in elenctic argument.

14   Nehamas is influenced by Pierre Hadot, who argues that philosophy in ancient times is a way of life and not a purely theoretical discipline (see Nehamas 1998: 164). From Nehamas's perspective, Vlastos is a paradigmatic theoretical philosopher. When Vlastos writes about Socratic irony, he seeks to get it right. All that matters is the quality of answers, not the nature of the person (Vlastos) who offers them.

15   There is a rough parallel between Nehamas's distinction between theoretical philosophy and philosophy as the art of living and Rorty's distinction between systematic philosophy and edifying philosophy. Nehamas writes:

> Systematic philosophers think of the philosophers of the art of living at best as "poets" or literary figures, or at worst as charlatans writing for precocious teenagers or, what for many amount to the same thing, for professors of literature. The philosophers of the art of living accuse systematic philosophers of being a misguided and self-deceived way of doing what they consider true philosophy to be. They think that its adherents are cowardly, dry pedants who desire scientific objectivity because they are unable to create a work that is truly their own and use disinterestedness and detachment to mask their own sterility. (Nehamas 1998: 4)

The above distinction not only parallels Rorty's distinction between systematic and edifying philosophers, but comes close to describing Rorty himself. Philosophers in the analytic tradition have accused Rorty of being a charlatan who writes for professors of literature. Moreover, Rorty seeks to unmask the pretense of neutral objectivity. He champions the self-creativity of poets. Nehamas thinks that both extremes are *mistaken*. "Both are wrong for the same reason. They both overlook the fact that each approach is a legitimate historical development of philosophy as it began in classical Greece; neither of these approaches has an exclusive hold on the essence of philosophy (which does not, in any case, exist)" (Nehamas 1998: 4).

Rorty was a great admirer of Nehamas's early book on Nietzsche. In *Contingency, Irony, Solidarity*, he writes: "My account of Nietzsche owes a great deal to Alexander Nehamas' original and penetrating *Nietzsche: Life as Literature*" (Rorty 1989: 27, n. 4). Rorty draws on Nehamas to present a reading of Nietzsche as engaging in ironical self-creation. Although Nehamas never cites Rorty in *The Art of Living*, it is clear from the way in which he describes aestheticist philosophers of the art of living that he has been influenced by Rorty. For example, (in a Rortian spirit) Nehamas writes: "The philosophers of the art of living I discuss in this book all consider the self to be not given but a constructed unity" (Nehamas 1998: 4).

16   Nehamas declares that there are three varieties of the art of living. All three involve irony. The first is exemplified by Socrates as he is portrayed in Plato's early dialogues.

> Practicing his art in public, and to that extent committed to his interlocutors' welfare, Socrates still cannot show that his mode of life is right for all. Convinced that it is, Socrates has no arguments to persuade others that his conviction is correct. He urges people to join him in the examined life he considers the only life worth living for a human being, but he has nothing to say when someone like Euthyphro simply walks away from their confrontation. His ideal may be universalist, but he has no means by which to prove that is right. He remains tentative and protreptic. (Nehamas 1998: 9)

A second genre of the art of living is found in Plato's middle works, especially the *Phaedo* and the *Republic*. Here Plato, still using Socrates as his main character, seeks to elaborate the *life of philosophy* – the mode of life that Plato claims is the best of all to live or to approximate. In the middle dialogues, Plato claims that "the life of philosophy as he defines it in detail in these works, is best for all, and he offers a series of controversial arguments in order to convince those who can do so to choose that life for themselves and those who can't to try to approximate it as closely as their abilities allow" (Nehamas 1998: 9).

The third genre is what Nehamas calls "aestheticist." It is exemplified by Montaigne, Nietzsche, and Foucault. In this genre, individuals create and construct themselves through a distinctive style of writing. In this third genre, there is no best work, no best life by which all the others can be judged. Nehamas, like Lear and Rorty (and unlike Plato of the middle dialogues) does not believe that there is a *single* type of life that can be designated as the *best* type of life for all.

The Art of Living consists of two parts. The first part, entitled "Silence," is concerned with analyzing the meaning of Platonic and Socratic irony. The second part, entitled "Voices," analyzes Montaigne, Nietzsche, and Foucault. My primary focus is on Part I, especially Nehamas's discussion of Socratic irony.

17   The different interpretations of Platonic irony are no less controversial than the debates about Socratic irony. Stanley Rosen writes: "*Only by the recognition of irony as the central problem in the interpretation of Plato, do we honor the demands of rigorous and sober philosophical analysis*" (Rosen 1967: p. xiv).

18   To support his reading of what Plato's irony seeks to achieve, Nehamas cites a passage from Michael Frede: "[T]o revise beliefs which are so deeply interwoven with the fabric of our life in such a way as to achieve

and maintain consistency is extremely difficult, in part because it means, or at least might mean, a basic change of life" (Nehamas 1998: 42). Frede makes a more general point about the relation of arguments to the dialogue form: "By their artful characterization of the dramatic context of the arguments, the dialogues show in an unsurpassable way how philosophy is tied to real life, to forms of life, to character and behavior" (Frede 1992: 216).

19   Compare Nehamas's criticism of Vlastos about how complex irony becomes transparent with a similar objection in Kierkegaard about irony as a figure of speech in *The Concept of Irony*.

> The ironic figure of speech cancels itself, however, inasmuch as the one who is speaking assumes that his hearers understand him, and thus, through a negation of the immediate phenomenon, the essence becomes identical with the phenomenon. If it sometimes happens that an ironic figure of speech such as this is misunderstood, this is not the fault of the one who is speaking, except insofar as he has come to grips with such a crafty fellow as irony, who likes to play tricks as much on friends as on foes. In fact, we say of such an ironic turn of speech: Its earnestness is not in earnest. The remark is so earnest that it is shocking, but the hearer in the know shares the secret lying behind it. But precisely thereby the irony is once again cancelled. It is the most common form of irony to say something earnestly that is not meant in earnest. The second form of irony, to say as a jest, jestingly, something that is meant in earnest, is more rare. But, as was mentioned, the ironic figure of speech cancels itself; it is like a riddle to which at the same time one has the solution. (Kierkegaard 1989: 248)

20   Nehamas also argues that Vlastos presents a misleading simplification of the views of Cicero and Quintilian. See Nehamas 1998: 54–6 for his interpretation of what Cicero and Quintilian mean by irony.
21   For another approach to Platonic and Socratic irony that is sympathetic to Nehamas's critique of Vlastos see Griswold 2002.
22   Nehamas is correct when he says that Vlastos wants to absolve Socrates of responsibility for Alcibiades' misunderstanding. Yet, when Vlastos actually describes the situation between Socrates and Alcibiades, he comes very close to Nehamas's description. See Vlastos 1991: 44. If Socrates knows that Alcibiades has gone wrong and doesn't "lift a finger" to dispel his error (as Vlastos maintains), it would appear that Socrates *does* indeed bear *some* responsibility for Alcibiades' mistake.
23   Any interpreter of Plato must confront the seeming paradox of how Socrates' profession of ignorance is compatible with his insistence that there are certain ethical principles that he accepts, such as the principle affirmed in the *Apology*, "that to do injustice and to disobey a superior, whether divine or human: that I know to be bad and shameful," and the principle Socrates affirms in the *Crito* (49c10–11) "one should never return injustice nor harm another human being, no matter what one

suffers at their hands." How can we understand Socrates' disavowal of knowledge when we are confronted with his claims to know that these things are true? Is he just contradicting himself? Or is the conflict, in some way or another, merely apparent? See Nehamas 1998: 72–87 for his discussion of this paradox – and for the reasons why he disagrees with Vlastos's interpretation.

24   Vlastos begins his discussion of Socratic irony by quoting Quintilian, that irony is a figure of speech "in which something contrary to what is said is to be understood" (Vlastos 1991: 21). This is the thesis that Nehamas criticizes. Nehamas is interpreting "contrary" in its strict, logical sense. When, however, Vlastos discusses what he means by "complex irony" – Socratic irony – it becomes clear that he doesn't quite mean "contrary" in this literal, strong sense. In his remarks on Socratic ignorance and teaching, Vlastos claims that the *sense* in which Socrates denies that he has knowledge and is not a teacher differs from the *sense* in which Socrates does have knowledge and is a teacher. But then, what is denied and what is affirmed are not logical contraries; they only *seem* to be contraries. In this respect, there is an analogy with Kant's antinomies, insofar as what initially seems to be contradictory turns out (when properly explicated and analyzed) not to be contradictory, but actually compatible.

25   Although both Lear and Nehamas cite Kierkegaard in order to clarify the meaning of Socratic irony, their interpretations of Kierkegaard are strikingly different. Lear, we recall, based his interpretation of irony on a single entry from Kierkegaard's journals dated Dec. 3, 1854. Nehamas's quotation is from *The Concept of Irony*, Kierkegaard's Magister dissertation. Lear is dismissive of this early academic work by Kierkegaard. He claims that, in his later works, Kierkegaard (or rather his pseudonymous author Johannes Climacus) rejects the early reflections on Socratic irony. Lear acknowledges that "Nehamas valuably distinguishes Platonic irony from Socratic irony and he makes apt criticisms of Vlastos' interpretation." But Lear also says: "However, in following Vlastos in his misplaced criticism of Kierkegaard, Nehamas misses what, from a Kierkegaardian perspective, makes irony such a philosophically and ethically powerful phenomenon" (Lear 2011: 184, n. 38).

26   Nehamas quotes an early passage from *The Concept of Irony* in which Kierkegaard writes much the same thing: "What Socrates himself prized so highly, namely standing still and contemplating – in other words, silence – this is his whole life in terms of world history. *And Kierkegaard is right*" (Nehamas 1998: 70, emphasis added).

27   To anticipate, Nehamas's depiction of Plato's Socrates comes very close to the way in which Kierkegaard described Socrates in *The Concept of Irony*. Andrew Cross, describing Kierkegaard's "radical verbal irony," which is the type of speech that Kierkegaard attributes to Socrates, writes:

To speak in this way is to say something that can be taken in a variety of ways, without intending the hearer to take it in any one of those ways. What is said could be taken as an expression that p or as an expression that $not\text{-}p$ or as an expression that q; and S is unconcerned as to which of these H takes this to be. He is interested only in producing these riddles; and since they are riddles, saying them does not commit him, in the sense that he cannot be held to account for having expressed that p or that $not\text{-}p$ or that q. *He was expressing, literally, nothing*; that the hearer takes him to be expressing something, intending to communicate something is the hearer's responsibility. (Cross 1998: 131, emphasis added)

28   The provocation to interpret and reinterpret Socrates is also the theme of Sarah Kofman's *Socrates: Fictions of a Philosopher.* She explores the interpretations of Hegel, Kierkegaard, and Nietzsche. See Kofman 1998.

29   Nehamas would endorse E. N. Tigerstedt's remarks on the responsibility of the reader of Plato's dialogues: "Nothing is a matter of course; everything can be called into question. To read Plato demands a far higher degree of vigilance and activity than any other philosopher asks for. Time after time, we are forced to make our choice, to decide how we should interpret what we are reading" (Tigerstedt 1977: 99).

30   Nehamas declares that the main question that interests him is: "How did Socrates manage to live as he did, how did he become who he was?" (Nehamas 1998: 95). After reviewing the history of trying to solve the Socratic problem, Nehamas stresses the importance of the German Romantics in emphasizing the significance of Plato's Socrates. Before the Romantics, Xenophon was taken to be the primary authority on the historical Socrates. "The real authority of Plato as the true source for the historical Socrates is the product of German Romanticism, and I am convinced that the importance of irony both to Plato and to the Romantics played a crucial role in that transformation" (Nehamas 1998: 94).

31   Nietzsche, of course, expresses a much more critical and ambivalent attitude toward Socrates.

32   In a critical discussion written shortly after the publication of Vlastos's book (and shortly after Vlastos's death) entitled "Voices of Silence: On Gregory Vlastos's Socrates," Nehamas succinctly states his disagreement with Vlastos, which he develops at greater length in *The Art of Living*.

Taking his [Socrates'] disavowals as complex ironies robs him of his strangeness and in fact eliminates his irony. Assuming, by contrast, that he was sincere supplies him with a much more profound ironical mask after all – a mask that it is difficult, if not impossible, to remove. For now he turns out to be someone who, precisely in disavowing ethical knowledge and the ability to provide it for others, succeeded in living as moral a life as anyone who belongs in the tradition he himself originated.

And he does not let us know how. This, in turn, is a profound instance of irony. For irony cannot simply be defined as Vlastos, following the tradition originating in Quintilian, defines it, as saying one thing and meaning the opposite – a definition that ultimately applies to complex irony as well. Often, irony consists in letting your audience know that something is taking place inside you that they simply are not allowed to see. But it also, more radically, leaves open the question whether you are seeing it yourself: speakers are not always in the privileged position in relation to themselves that Quintilian attributes to them. Irony often communicates the fact that the audience is not getting the whole picture; but it does not necessarily imply that the speaker has that picture or that, indeed, there is a whole picture to be understood in the first place. (Nehamas 1999a: 102–3)

33   Nehamas claims that Socrates' main accomplishment is that "he established a new way of life, a new art of living," but that Plato's early dialogues do not make clear the "exact connection between the views one holds and the life one leads." According to Nehamas, it is in the middle dialogues, especially in the *Republic*, that Plato "produces a grandiose set of considerations to show that the life of philosophy – inspired by the life of Socrates but not strictly identical with it – is really the best for everyone, philosophers and non-philosophers alike" (Nehamas 1998: 96).

34   I have focused on the competing interpretations of Socratic irony by Vlastos and Nehamas because many of the philosophical issues concerning the significance of irony for living a human life are in the foreground of their discussion. But, as I indicated earlier, the literature of Socratic irony – especially since the time of German Romanticism – is immense. This literature contains different, conflicting, and frequently contradictory accounts of Socratic irony.

35   This is the definition of irony in Webster's dictionary that Vlastos cites to show that Quintilian's formula for irony has "stood the test of time" (Vlastos 1991: 21). Nehamas agrees that "complex irony" – as Vlastos describes it – exists; but this is not an adequate characterization of Socratic irony. "There is no question that the version of irony Vlastos describes surely exists – even children, as he writes, do it" (Nehamas 1998: 53).

Chapter 3   Søren Kierkegaard: Irony and Ethical Passion

1   I do not think that Vlastos fairly represents what Kierkegaard means by deception and its ironic significance. In *The Point of View* (published posthumously) Kierkegaard writes:

But from a total point of view of my whole work as an author, the esthetic writing is a deception, and herein is the deeper significance of the *pseudonymity*. But a deception, that is indeed something rather ugly. To that I would answer: Do not be deceived by the word *deception*. One can deceive a person out of what is true, and one – to recall old Socrates – can deceive a person into what is true. Yes, in only this way can a deluded person actually be brought into what is true – by deceiving him…What then, does it mean to "deceive"? It means that one does not begin *directly* with what one wishes to communicate but begins by taking the other's delusion at face value. (Kierkegaard 1998: 53–4)

This is what Socrates does over and over again in the Socratic dialogues. As we have seen in the discussion of the *Euthyphro*, Socrates begins by taking Euthyphro's claims at "face value." Socrates uses irony as a technique to expose Euthyphro's *delusion*. Socrates is not deceiving his interlocutors in the sense of *misleading* them or causing them to believe what is not true. Rather, the function of his irony and elenctic encounters is to get his interlocutors to abandon the illusions and delusions to which they cling.

2   In rejecting Quintilian's notion that Socratic irony is nothing but feigned ignorance, Nehamas is also criticizing Vlastos. More generally, Nehamas, like Kierkegaard, rejects all those interpreters of Plato's early dialogues who understand them as a form of *didactic* dialectic, whereby a "questioner who knows the answer to a question of which the respondent is ignorant brings that respondent to the necessary knowledge by means of a series of cleverly designed questions" (Nehamas 1998: 72).

3   There is even a danger in relying on the posthumously published *The Point of View* as a guide to how to read Kierkegaard's writings. For a discussion of some of the inconsistencies and problems with taking *The Point of View* as authoritative, see Garff 2002 and Schönbaumsfeld 2007: 61–8.

4   In "Putting Two and Two Together: Kierkegaard, Wittgenstein and the Point of View for their Work as Authors," Conant makes an insightful remark in an endnote. He writes:
    "The views expressed in a pseudonymous work are to be attributed not to Kierkegaard but to the literary character who voices them – a literary character who the work as a whole, in turn, brings to life for us. So we have therefore one sense in which Kierkegaard does not 'directly communicate' any views of his own through such a work" (Conant 1995: 307, n. 28).
    With a few appropriate substitutions, we have the precise view that Nehamas ascribes to Plato's early dialogues. We can reformulate Conant's statement as follows:
    "The views expressed in [the early dialogues] are to be attributed not to [Plato] but to a literary character who voices them – a literary

character [Socrates] who the work as a whole, in turn brings to life for us. So we have here therefore one sense in which [Plato] does not 'directly communicate' any views of his own through such a work."

There is another passage about Kierkegaard in Conant's article that echoes Nehamas's distinction between theoretical philosophy and philosophy as the art of living. It places Kierkegaard squarely in the tradition of thinkers concerned with the fashioning and care of the self.

> To be a modern philosopher is to be concerned with what can be doubted through a purely intellectual effort, regardless of what can actually be doubted in the context of one's everyday life. As Kierkegaard sees it, the ancients took philosophy to consist in a practical activity (of moulding the self), while the moderns take it to consist in a theoretical activity (of subjecting a set of beliefs to critical scrutiny). For the ancients, philosophy had its telos in the sphere of the ethical (in the practical task of disciplining the passions, shaping the self, and transforming its mode of existence), whereas the moderns (often unwittingly) confine philosophy to the sphere of the aesthetic – specifically to the sphere of doctrine and the intellectual task of assessing the truth or falsity of various propositions. (Conant 1995: 315, n. 38).

Conant's interpretation of Kierkegaard (and Wittgenstein) is extremely controversial. For a discussion and critique of Conant's claims about Kierkegaard, see Schönbaumsfeld 2007: 85–154 and Lippitt 2000: 47–71.

5   I speak of "highlights" because I am certainly not attempting to provide a comprehensive discussion of everything that Kierkegaard and his pseudonymous authors have to say about irony and Socrates. The notes and supplements to the Hongs' edition of *The Concept of Irony* help to relate key passages to some of the other discussions of Socratic irony in Kierkegaard's journals and in his pseudonymous writings.

6   This fifteenth thesis succinctly states what Lear takes to be the essential connection between irony and living a human life. See also the following passage near the end of *The Concept of Irony*: "Just as scientists maintain that there is no true science without doubt, so it may be maintained with the same right that no genuinely human life is possible without irony" (Kierkegaard 1989: 326). Although Lear cites this passage, he doesn't explore the meaning of irony in *The Concept of Irony*. For an imaginative interpretation of Kierkegaard's fifteen theses, see Kofman 1998: 130–3. She writes: "Notwithstanding the fact, then, that the fifteen 'theses' were written in Latin, with the utmost seriousness, they still helped to undermine the seriousness of the *Thesis* and the university as an institution, at the outset; moreover, appearances to the contrary, they enabled Kierkegaard to make sport of his jury and its verdict" (Kofman 1998; 133).

7   Paul de Man, probing irony as a literary trope, claims that irony properly understood calls into question the possibility of defining irony in

conceptual terms. Irony upsets the stability of all concepts. See de Man 1996.

8 Earlier commentators on *The Concept of Irony* claimed that the dissertation was self-consciously written as an ironic attack on Hegel and the Danish Hegelians; but more recent commentators stress a more nuanced use and critique of Hegel and Danish Hegelians. For a succinct review of the debates about the anti-Hegelian reading of *The Concept of Irony* see Söderquist 2013: 4–7. Although Jon Stewart expresses some skepticism about whether the structure of *The Concept of Irony* is Hegelian, he claims: "One can see *The Concept of Irony* as a sort of commentary on a part of Hegel's *Lectures on the History of Philosophy*. When one looks at Hegel's table of contents for the relevant section, one can map Kierkegaard's analyses here in the dissertation onto it in a fairly straightforward manner" (Stewart 2003: 177).

9 Both Vlastos and Kierkegaard agree that if Xenophon were our sole source of information about Socrates, we would never know that Socrates was an ironist.

10 "Therefore, even though we lack direct evidence about Socrates, even though we lack an altogether reliable view of him, we do have in recompense all the various nuances of misunderstanding, and in my opinion this our best asset with a personality such as Socrates" (Kierkegaard 1989: 128).

11 See Söderquist's lucid account of Hegel's Socrates, which he contrasts with Kierkegaard's Socrates, in Söderquist 2013: 59–74.

12 In his *Encyclopedia Logic*, Hegel describes Socratic irony in a similar manner: "Socrates' irony was to pretend in his conversations that he wanted to be instructed more precisely about the matter under discussion; and in this connection, he raised all manner of questions so that the people with whom he conversed were led to say the opposite of what had appeared to them at the beginning to be correct" (Hegel 1991: 129).

13 Söderquist calls Kierkegaard's depiction of Socrates' ironic world view "nihilism." Although "nihilism" is not a word that Kierkegaard uses in *The Concept of Irony*, Söderquist claims that the expression "captures a *radical* feature of Kierkegaard's thought... [T]he ironical consciousness embodied by Socrates and later discussed as 'pure irony' is radically 'empty,' 'negative' and 'destructive' precisely when it comes to the question of practical principles" (Söderquist 2013: 24, n. 1).

14 Sylviane Agacinski makes this point emphatically when she writes: "In brief: Kierkegaard refuses to grant Socrates any kind of positivity; Socrates has no point of view outside irony, his attitude is infinitely subjective and infinitely negative regarding every positivity; he is incapable of 'positing' anything, at least as long as he sees his *point de vue* to the bitter end" (Agacinski 1988: 34).

15   Kierkegaard's swerve away from Hegel helps to make sense of another point that Kierkegaard emphasizes in *The Concept of Irony* (and in many of his other writings): the distinction between inner state and outer behavior (or action). In many places, Hegel insists on the identity of the internal and the external. In his *Encyclopedia Logic*, he categorically states: "Hence what is only something inner is also thereby external and what is only external is also something inner" (Hegel 1991: 210). For Kierkegaard, the very condition for the *possibility* of irony presupposes a sharp distinction between inner and outer. We cannot tell what is inner on the basis of the outward speech and deeds of Socrates.

16   See John Lippitt's illuminating discussion of the meaning and significance of Socrates as *exemplar*. Although Lippitt is primarily concerned with Johannes Climacus's discussion of Socrates in *Concluding Unscientific Postscript*, much of what he says is applicable to the depiction of Socrates in *The Concept of Irony* (Lippitt 2000: 42–5).

17   Despite Kierkegaard's attempt to differentiate what he is saying from Hegel, his very language echoes the Hegelian idiom. This is illustrated in phrases like "the service of the idea" and his references to "ideality."

18   Söderquist labels this "the isolated self," which is the title of his book about *The Concept of Irony*. Although I am in sympathy with his existential reading of the book – and especially his subtle discussion of the differences between Hegel's and Kierkegaard's portrayal of Socrates – I am *not* persuaded by his major thesis that "Kierkegaard insists that only 'the religious' can transubstantiate the finite world which has lost its content through the critical gaze of irony" (Söderquist 2013: 200). Despite Söderquist's careful reconstruction of the debates about irony that were taking place when Kierkegaard wrote his dissertation, I don't see that Kierkegaard offers any *arguments* in *The Concept of Irony* to show "that only 'the religious' can transubstantiate the finite world."

19   Kevin Newmark captures this point when he writes: "Irony as negativity characterizes the coming of consciousness of subjectivity through the subject's original capacity to turn away from – and therefore to negate – all else, including its own propensity for error as natural consciousness" (Newmark 2012: 44).

20   For Kierkegaard's critical comments about *The Concept of Irony* see the Hongs' "Historical Introduction" to *The Concept of Irony* (Kierkegaard 1989: pp. vi–xxv). See also Stewart 2003: 141–4.

21   For a recent discussion of Hegel's critique of Romantic irony, see Reid 2014.

22   Despite Lear's claim that Kierkegaard is his teacher, he fails to follow Kierkegaard in *emphasizing* the double-edged quality of irony. Irony may be necessary for living a human life, but it can also destroy a human life. In this respect, Rorty is more sensitive to Kierkegaard's point when he stresses how irony can be cruel and can also humiliate.

23 Consider two attempts to make sense of what Kierkegaard calls "irony as a controlled element." Brad Frazier claims that irony is properly mastered through "moral commitment," and that this commitment is broadly construed "as an ultimate commitment to the good of persons in general and to goodness and moral obligation" (Frazier 2006: 133). I find no textual evidence in *The Concept of Irony* to support such claims. If we take Kierkegaard's portrayal of Socrates as the ironist seriously – with his relentless negativity – then what Frazier describes as "irony as properly mastered" turns out to be the abandonment of irony.

Söderquist gives a perceptive description of what Kierkegaard *intends*:

> The ironist, whether it be Socrates or a romantic ironist, cannot take seriously the values of his or her cultural environment, and ends up cynically refusing to identify him- or herself with any of the practical ends and goals of the human community. He or she therefore stands alone. While Kierkegaard sees a healthy skepticism in this world-view, he also *argues* that in the end, the isolation of irony must be overcome; the ironist must be able to take ownership of the concrete relationships in which he or she find him- or herself. (Söderquist 2013: 173, emphasis added)

My disagreement with Söderquist concerns one word, "argues." Kierkegaard certainly *asserts* that isolation must be overcome and that one needs to take ownership of concrete relationships, but he does not present any *arguments* in *The Concept of Irony* to support this claim. Kierkegaard leaves us in a serious bind because, given his reiterated emphatic insistence on the radical negativity of the ironist, it is impossible to see how the isolation of the ironist can be overcome, how the ironist can achieve any *positive* commitment.

24 I have already indicated that in "A First and Last Declaration" (signed by Kierkegaard at the end of *Concluding Unscientific Postscript*), he requests that anyone citing remarks from his pseudonymous authors should attribute the remarks to them and not to him. But there is plenty of evidence that the views on irony expressed in *Concluding Unscientific Postscript* are also the views of Kierkegaard. See Lippitt 2000, Cross 1998, and Westphal 1996.

25 Even in *The Concept of Irony*, Kierkegaard declares: "But irony is the beginning and yet no more than the beginning" (Kierkegaard 1989: 214).

26 Lippitt makes a similar point in his discussion of *Concluding Unscientific Postscript*:

> [T]here are two 'ironist' figures in that text: the 'mere' [pure] ironist and the figure portrayed as being 'really' an ethicist, but who uses irony as his 'incognito'. Climacus, it seems, would condemn the former as being 'negative', in roughly the sense of that term used in *The Concept of Irony*; such an ironist has no 'way out'; while he recognizes the deficiencies of immediacy, he has nothing to offer in its place. By contrast the ethicist

who uses irony as his incognito has what is, in Climacus' schema, a more complete picture: he is aware of, and is continually appropriating the ethical's demand. This realization of the ethical's demand is his way out. (Lippitt 2000: 145)

27 There is a new English translation of *Philosophical Fragments* entitled *Philosophical Crumbs*. M. G. Piety explains the rationale for this new title: "The Danish word '*Smuler*' means 'bits, scraps, crumbs, or trifles'. For years it has been translated in English as 'fragments'. But 'fragments' is not among the dictionary's favoured options for '*Smuler*', and it guarantees that the nimble irony of that topsy-turvy title is lost" (Kierkegaard 2009: p. xvi).

28 Andrew Cross points out that in another place in the *Postscript*, Climacus places irony between immediacy and the ethical. Cross presents an illuminating discussion of the different senses of immediacy in Kierkegaard and how the aesthetic is related to immediacy (Cross 1998: 136–7; 142–7).

29 Speaking of the ethical as an "existence-sphere" helps to elucidate what Kierkegaard means by "the ethical." As a distinctive sphere, Kierkegaard is emphasizing the basic attitude, the basic way of being oriented in the world that enables one to make specific concrete existential ethical decisions and choices. Consequently, ethical passion fully emerges only in this ethical existence-sphere. In the "purely" aesthetic, there are no *ethical* choices and decisions, because the *continuity of self* that is required for ethical passion is lacking.

30 In the *Encyclopedia Logic*, Hegel states: "Hence what is only something inner is also thereby external, and what is only external is also only something inner" (Hegel 1991: 210).

31 In his discussion of irony, Climacus declares: "Most people live in the opposite way. They are busy with being something when someone is watching them. If possible, they are something in their own eyes as soon as others are watching them, but inwardly, where the absolute requirement is watching them, they have no taste for accentuating the personal *I*" (Kierkegaard 1992: 503).

32 Despite Kierkegaard's emphasis on the single individual, he is fully aware that single individuals are *social* and belong to *communities*. That is why irony is essentially dialogical. His objection to Hegel is that in emphasizing (exaggerating) the role of the state for ethical life, Hegel diminishes the ethical significance of the single individuals who constitute a community.

33 Söderquist also notes these two stages or movements of irony.

> Kierkegaard describes "irony" as a consciousness that cultivates isolation from the world of inherited values, an isolation which, in the first instance, Kierkegaard considers to be *necessary* for the development of the self. Insofar as the ironic consciousness recognizes that the self is essentially

different from the cultural environment in which it resides, it contains a "truth." Ironic isolation, however is also a potential hindrance to self-hood, he says, since the self can only be realized in the unique finite circumstances in which it finds itself, for it is in dialogue with finitude that one realizes the "primitive" or "original" self, the divinely posited self. Ironic isolation is thus also "untruth." The isolated ironic conscious-ness must make a second movement if it is to escape irony and become a self: it must move back toward finitude again. In Kierkegaard's terminology, the isolated self must become "reconciled with actuality." (Söderquist 2013: 2–3)

My disagreement with Söderquist concerns two points. First, although Kierkegaard says something like this in *The Concept of Irony*, he clarifies this "second movement" only in *Concluding Unscientific Postscript*. Second, this "second movement" is not an escape from irony, it is the fulfillment of irony – the "truth of irony" that demands a passing beyond abstract or "pure irony."

34 In *The Point of View*, Kierkegaard gives one of his clearest justifications of the need for indirect discourse. Although he is speaking about Chris-tendom, his key point is just as relevant to Socratic irony. "No, an illu-sion can never be removed directly, and basically only indirectly…That is, one who is under an illusion must be approached from behind…By a direct attack he only strengthens a person in the illusion and also infuriates him" (Kierkegaard 1998: 43).

35 For a thorough discussion of what it means to *become* a self in *Concluding Unscientific Postscript*, see Westphal 1996.

36 There has been a tendency by both defenders and critics of Kierkegaard to emphasize that he is a radically individualist thinker who has little sense of the significance of the social and communal character of indi-viduals. Kierkegaard was certainly a sharp critic of what he took to be a tendency of his times to favor an anonymous mass public in which single individuals are submerged. But recent scholars have challenged this reading of Kierkegaard. They have argued that Kierkegaard has a *positive* concept of community, wherein existing individuals flourish and recognize their ethical responsibility by caring for other human beings. For a discussion of the role that irony plays in issues concerning social justice and politics, see Williams 2012. For a discussion of the rela-tionship of the individual to society (and community), see Matuštik 1993, Matuštik and Westphal 1995, and also Morgan 2012.

Chapter 4   Irony, Philosophy, and Living a Human Life

1 The quotations from Descartes in this passage are from Descartes 1969: 149, 198–9.

2 For a balanced evaluation of the revelations in Heidegger's recently published, *Black Notebooks*, see Gordon 2014.
3 In his Introduction to *Socrates: Ironist and Moral Philosopher*, subtitled "How This Book Came to Be," Vlastos explains how he came to this understanding of Socrates' disavowal of knowledge by correcting an error he had made earlier.

> [Socrates] asserts that he has no knowledge, none whatsoever, not a smidgen of it, "no wisdom, great or small" (Ap. 21B–D). But he speaks and lives, serenely confident that he has a goodly stock of it – sufficient for the quotidian pursuit of virtue. And he *implies* as much in what he says. To keep faith with Socrates' strangeness, some way has to be found to save both the assertion of ignorance and the implied negation. My mistake – explicit in the Introduction to the *Protagoras*, implicit in "The Paradox of Socrates" – had been to accept the assertion and ignore the balancing reservations. I had maintained: "he had seen [1] that his investigative method's aim cannot be final demonstrative certainty, and [2] that its practice is quite compatible with suspended judgment as to the material truth of any of its conclusions (Vlastos, 1956: p. xxxi). [1] is exactly right and it goes to the heart of what is ground-breakingly new in Socrates. What I had said to this effect – placing Socratic renunciation of epistemic certainty at the core of his philosophizing – was one of the best things in that introduction. But it was wrong to conjoin with it claim [2]. There is no necessary connection. John Dewey was not giving up the search for knowledge when making the quest for certainty his *bête noire*. Neither was Socrates in *his* disclaimer of certainty – he least of all philosophers, maintaining as he did that knowledge *is* virtue. My error had been to saddle Socrates with [2] on the strength of nothing better than [1]. (Vlastos 1991: 3–4)

4 Vlastos's identification of "justified true belief" with what is "justifiable through the peculiarly Socratic method of elenctic argument" implies a very *weak* sense of "justified true belief." The Socrates of the early Platonic dialogues engages in elenctic argument with only a very few interlocutors, none of whom are Socrates' equal in producing arguments.
5 For Kahn's detailed critique of Vlastos's claims about elenctic knowledge and the role it plays in Plato's dialogues see Kahn 1992: 244–53.
6 See also Nehamas's and Lear's critical discussions of elenchus in Nehamas 1998: 82–5 and Lear 2005: 456–60.
7 Lear makes a similar point when he writes: "But when one asks what method Socrates used, the answer that typically comes to mind – the famous method of cross-examination, the elenchus – seems unsatisfying...[I]f one looks at the dialogues in which elenchus is used, there is no evidence that any of the interlocutors are improved by the conversation" (Lear 2005: 442).
8 In a footnote commenting on the Greek word that is translated as "strangeness," Vlastos writes: "ἀτοπία. The Greek is stronger;

'strangeness' picks it up at the lower end of its intensity-range. At the higher end 'outrageousness' or even 'absurdity' would be required to match its force" (Vlastos 1991: 1).

9　Nehamas succinctly states his disagreement with Vlastos about Socrates – and more generally about irony.

> I argue – against the common view, exemplified in Gregory Vlastos' own reflection on Socrates – that irony does not consist in saying the contrary of, but only something different from, what one means. In the former case, if we know that we are faced with irony we also know what the ironist means: all we need to do is to negate the words we hear in order to understand what the ironist has in mind. In the latter, even when we know that we are confronted with irony, we have no sure way of knowing the ironist's meaning: all we know is that it is not quite what we heard. Irony therefore does not allow us to peer into the ironist's mind, which remains concealed and inscrutable. Socratic irony is of that kind. It does not ever indicate what he thinks: it leaves us with his words and a doubt that they express his meaning. That is why I think of Socratic irony as a form of silence. (Nehamas 1998: 12)

10　Lear also thinks that both Nehamas and Vlastos are to be faulted for their "misplaced criticism of Kierkegaard. Nehamas misses what, from a Kierkegaardian perspective, makes irony such a philosophically and ethically powerful phenomenon" (Lear 2011: 184, n. 38). See also Lear 2005: 461, n. 25 for further criticisms of Vlastos and Nehamas.

11　Recently, it has become fashionable to argue that what many standard interpreters take to be straightforward claims in texts are really intended as ironical. The purpose of the irony in these texts is therapeutic – to cure us of the philosophical illusions that entrap us. James Conant and Cora Diamond have argued that this is the proper way to read Wittgenstein's *Tractatus*. They argue that the frame of the *Tractatus* (the Preface and the famous penultimate "proposition," 6.54) provides the essential clue for a correct reading. When Wittgenstein declares in 6.54 that "my propositions serve as elucidations in the following way: anyone who understands me eventually recognizes them as nonsensical," he means that they are *plain* nonsense – not "substantial nonsense" or "interesting nonsense." Conant also makes similar claims about Kierkegaard's *Concluding Unscientific Postscript*. See the articles by Conant and Diamond in Crary and Read 2000. For Conant's comparison between Wittgenstein and Kierkegaard, see Conant 1993 and 1995. For critiques of Conant's interpretation of Kierkegaard, see Lippitt 2000 and Schönbaumsfeld 2007.

12　One of the reasons why Rorty was attracted to the work of the later Wittgenstein is because of Wittgenstein's consistent critique of the idea that philosophy is a special discipline that yields theses and doctrines.

13   Rorty would prefer to say that he is not advancing a philosophical thesis, but rather is showing us that in his "redescription" there is no place for even raising the issue of this kind of rational justification.

14   See Bernstein 1991: 258–92.

15   Along with John Dewey, William James was one of Rorty's heroes. Rorty's critique of Philosophy with a capital "P" and his description of irony are close in spirit to the way in which James characterized his radical pluralism.

> It is curious how little countenance radical pluralism has ever had among philosophers. Whether materialistically or spiritualistically minded, philosophers have always aimed at clearing up the litter with which the world is apparently filled. They have substituted economical and orderly conceptions for the first sensible tangle, and whether these were morally elevated or only intellectually neat, they were at any rate always aesthetically pure and definite, and aimed at ascribing to the world something clean and intellectual in the way of inner structure. As compared with these rationalizing pictures, the pluralistic empiricism which I profess offers a sorry appearance. It is a turbid, muddled, gothic sort of an affair, without sweeping outline and with little pictorial nobility. Those of you who are accustomed to the classical constructions of reality may be excused if your first reaction upon it be absolute contempt – a shrug of the shoulders, as if such ideas were unworthy of explicit refutation. But one must have lived some time with a system to appreciate its merits. Perhaps a little more familiarity may mitigate your first surprise at such a program as I offer. (James 1977: 26)

16   At times, Rorty comes close to acknowledging what I call "horizontal justification," although he insists on calling it "circular justification." This becomes evident if we insert "horizontal justification" in a passage that I previously quoted – one in which Rorty speaks about John Dewey, Michael Oakeshott, and John Rawls. Rorty writes: "All three would happily grant that a [horizontal justification] of our practices, a justification which makes one feature of our culture look good by citing still another, or comparing our culture invidiously with others by reference to our standards, is the only sort of justification we are going to get" (Rorty 1989: 57). For a further discussion of "horizontal justification" as it pertains to Rorty, see Bernstein 2006.

17   In "The Need for a Recovery of Philosophy," Dewey wrote: "Philosophy recovers itself when it ceases to be a device for dealing with the problems of philosophers and becomes a method cultivated by philosophers for dealing with the problems of men" (Dewey 1981: 95).

18   Söderquist shows that there was an intense discussion of irony (and humor) in Denmark at the time that Kierkegaard wrote his dissertation. Kierkegaard was aware of this discussion and presupposes it in his early investigation of irony. See ch. 6, "Irony, Humor, and the Religious Self," in Söderquist 2013: 173–200.

19 See my discussion of Arendt's distinction between knowledge and thinking in Bernstein 2000.

20 Arendt's description of how thinking is taught bears a strong resemblance to how irony is instilled. Quoting a passage from the *Meno*, she writes:

> "[T]he electric ray paralyzes others only through being paralyzed itself. It isn't that, knowing the answers myself I perplex other people. *The truth is rather that I infect them also with the perplexity I feel myself.*" Which, of course, sums up neatly the only way thinking can be taught – except that Socrates, as he repeatedly said, did not teach anything for the simple reason that he had nothing to teach; he was "sterile" like the midwives in Greece who were beyond the age of childbearing. (Arendt 1971: 431–2, emphasis added)

21 There is a crucial ambiguity in the phrase "to become human." It may suggest that there is a *single* essence to being human, and a *single* path to becoming human. But Kierkegaard is as much of an anti-essentialist as is Rorty. There is no one essence that defines our humanity, and there is no one way to become a human self. This is a choice and a decision that each "single individual" must make for herself. I think that it is clear – especially when he relates irony to the practice of psychoanalysis – that Lear agrees with the claim that there is no *one* way to become human.

22 Hilary Putnam makes a related point when he was asked: What makes a good philosopher? He responded that one should recognize that there are many different types of good philosopher. But then he went on to add: "If one has to generalize, I would agree with Myles Burnyeat, who once said that philosophy needs vision and arguments. Burnyeat's point was that there is something disappointing about a philosophy that contains arguments, however good, which are not inspired by some genuine vision, and something disappointing about a philosophic work that contains a vision, however inspiriting, which is unsupported by arguments" (Putnam 1999: 44).

References

Agacinski, S. (1988) *Aparté: Conceptions and Deaths of Søren Kierkegaard*. Florida State University Press, Tallahassee.

Ahbel-Rappe, S. and Kamtekar, R. (eds.) (2005) *A Companion to Socrates*. Blackwell, Oxford.

Arendt, H. (1971) Thinking and Moral Considerations: A Lecture. *Social Research* 38/3, pp. 417–46.

Auxier, R. E. and Hahn, L. E. (eds.) (2010) *The Philosophy of Richard Rorty*. Open Court, Chicago.

Bernstein, R. J. (1983) *Beyond Objectivism and Relativism: Science, Hermeneutics, and Praxis*. University of Pennsylvania Press, Philadelphia.

—— (1986) *Philosophical Profiles*. University of Pennsylvania Press, Philadelphia.

—— (1991) *The New Constellation: The Ethical-Political Horizon of Modernity/Postmodernity*. Polity, Cambridge.

—— (2000) Arendt on Thinking. In Villa (ed.) 2000, pp. 277–92.

—— (2003) Rorty's Inspirational Liberalism. In Guignon, and Hiley (eds.) 2003, pp. 124–38.

—— (2006) Can We Justify Universal Moral Norms? In Browning (ed.) 2006, pp. 3–17.

—— (2010) *The Pragmatic Turn*. Polity, Cambridge.

—— (2014) "So Much the Worse for your Old Intuitions, Start Working up some New Ones." *Contemporary Pragmatism* 11/4, pp. 5–14.

Booth, W. C. (1974) *A Rhetoric of Irony*. University of Chicago Press, Chicago.

Brandom, R. (ed.) (2000) *Rorty and his Critics*. Blackwell, Oxford.

—— (2000a) Vocabularies of Pragmatism: Synthesizing Naturalism and Historicism. In Brandom (ed.) 2000, pp. 156–83.

Brooks, C. (1947) *The Well Wrought Urn: Studies in the Structure of Poetry*. Harcourt Brace, New York.

Browning, D. (ed.) (2006) *Universalism vs. Relativism*. Rowman & Littlefield, New York.

Cohen, T., Guyer, P. and Putnam, H. (eds.) (1993) *Pursuits of Reason*. Texas University Press, Lubbock.

Colebrook, C. (2004) *Irony*. Routledge, New York.

Conant, J. (1993) Kierkegaard, Wittgenstein and Nonsense. In Cohen, Guyer, and Putnam (eds.) (1993), pp. 195–224.

—— (1995) Putting Two and Two Together: Kierkegaard, Wittgenstein and their Point of View for their Work as Authors. In Tessin and Ruhr (eds.) 1995, pp. 248–331.

Conway, D. and Gover, K. E. (eds.) (2002) *Søren Kierkegaard – Critical Assessments of Leading Philosophers*. Routledge, London.

Crary, A. and Read, R. (eds.) (2000) *The New Wittgenstein*. Routledge, London.

Cross, A. (1998) Neither Either nor Or: The Perils of Reflexive Irony. In Hannay and Marino (eds.) 1998, pp. 125–53.

de Man, P. (1996) The Concept of Irony. In P. de Man, *Aesthetic Ideology*, ed. A. Warminski. University of Minnesota Press, Minneapolis, pp. 163–84.

Descartes, R. (1969) *The Philosophical Works of Descartes*, 2 vols. trans. E. S. Haldane and G. R. T. Ross. Cambridge University Press, Cambridge.

Dewey, J. (1981) *The Philosophy of John Dewey*, ed. J. J. McDermott. University of Chicago Press, Chicago.

Frazier, B. (2006) *Rorty and Kierkegaard on Irony and Moral Commitment: Philosophical and Theological Reflections*. Palgrave Macmillan, New York.

Frede, M. (1992) Plato's Arguments and the Dialogue Form. *Oxford Studies in Ancient Philosophy*, Supplementary Volume, pp. 202–19.

Frye, N. (1957) *Anatomy of Criticism*. Princeton University Press, Princeton.

Garff, J. (2002) The Eyes of Argus – The Point of View and Points of View with Respect to Kierkegaard's "Activity as an Author." In Conway and Gover (eds.) 2002, pp. 71–96.

Gordon, P. E. (2014) Heidegger in Black. *New York Review of Books* (October 19), pp. 26–8.

Griswold, C. L. (2002) Irony in the Platonic Dialogues. *Philosophy and Literature* 26, pp. 84–106.

Guignon, C. and Hiley, D. R. (eds.) (2003) *Richard Rorty*. Cambridge University Press, Cambridge.

Hadot, P. (2002) *What is Ancient Philosophy?* Harvard University Press, Cambridge, Mass.

Hannay, A. and Marino, G. D. (eds.) (1998) *The Cambridge Companion to Kierkegaard*. Cambridge University Press, Cambridge.

Hegel, G. W. F. (1968) *Lectures on the History of Philosophy*, trans. E. S. Haldane and F. H. Simon. Routledge & Kegan Paul, London.

—— (1977) *The Phenomenology of Spirit*, trans. A. V. Miller. Clarendon Press, Oxford.

—— (1991) *Encyclopedia Logic. Part One of the Encyclopedia of the Philosophical Sciences*, trans. T. F. Geraets, W. A. Suchting, and H. S. Harris. Hackett, Indianapolis.

James, W. (1977) *A Pluralistic Universe*. Harvard University Press, Cambridge, Mass.

Jaspers, K. (1962) *Socrates, Buddha, Confucius, Christ: The Paradigmatic Individuals*, ed. H. Arendt. Harcourt, Brace and World, New York.

Kahn, C. H. (1992) Vlastos's Socrates, *Phronesis* 37/2, pp. 233–58.

—— (1996) *Plato and the Socratic Dialogue: The Philosophical Use of a Literary Form*. Cambridge University Press, Cambridge.

Kierkegaard, S. (1960) *The Diary of Søren Kierkegaard*, ed. P. P. Rohde. Citadel, New York.

—— (1989) *The Concept of Irony with Continual Reference to Socrates*, trans. H. V. Hong and E. H. Hong. Princeton University Press, Princeton.

—— (1992) *Concluding Unscientific Postscript to Philosophical Fragments*, trans. H. V. Hong and E. H. Hong. Princeton University Press, Princeton.

—— (1992a) *Either/Or*, trans. A. Hannay. Penguin Books, London.

—— (1998) *The Point of View*, trans. H. V. Hong and E. H. Hong. Princeton University Press, Princeton.

—— (2009) *Repetition and Philosophical Crumbs*, trans. M. G. Piety. Oxford University Press. Oxford.

Kofman, S. (1998) *Socrates: Fictions of a Philosopher*, trans. C. Porter. Cornell University Press, Ithaca.

Lear, J. (2005) The Socratic Method and Psychoanalysis. In Ahbel-Rappe and Kamtekar (eds.) 2005, pp. 442–62.

—— (2006) *Radical Hope: Ethics in the Face of Radical Devastation*. Harvard University Press, Cambridge, Mass.

—— (2011) *A Case for Irony*. Harvard University Press, Cambridge, Mass.

Lear, J. and MacIntyre, A. (2012) Irony and Humanity: A Dialogue between Jonathan Lear and Alasdair MacIntyre. www.hup.harvard.edu/.../irony-and-humanity/

Lippitt, J. (2000) *Humour and Irony in Kierkegaard's Thought*. Macmillan, London.

Matuštik, M. (1993) *Postnational Identity: Critical Theory and Existential Philosophy in Habermas, Kierkegaard, and Havel*. Guilford Press, New York.

Matuštik, M. and Westphal, M. (eds.) (1995) *Kierkegaard in Post/Modernity*. Indiana University Press, Bloomington.

Morgan, M. (2012) *Kierkegaard and Critical Theory*. Lexington Books, New York.

Muecke, D. C. (1969) *The Compass of Irony*. Methuen & Co., London.

Nehamas, A. (1998) *The Art of Living: Socratic Reflections from Plato to Foucault*. University of California Press, Berkeley.

—— (1999) *Virtues of Authenticity: Essays on Plato and Socrates*. Princeton University Press, Princeton.

—— (1999a) Voices of Silence: On Gregory Vlastos's Socrates. In Nehamas 1999, pp. 83–107.

Newmark, K. (2012) *Irony on Occasion: From Schlegel and Kierkegaard to Derrida and de Man*. Fordham University Press, New York.

Nietzsche, F. W. (1989) *Beyond Good and Evil*, trans. W. Kaufman. Vintage, New York.

Plato (1989) *Symposium of Plato*, trans. T. Griffith. University of California Press, Berkeley.

—— (1997) *Complete Works*, ed. J. M. Cooper. Hackett, Indianapolis.

Putnam, H. (1990) *Realism with a Human Face*. Harvard University Press, Cambridge, Mass.

—— (1999) Hilary Putnam: The Vision and Arguments of a Famous Harvard Philosopher (Interview). In Pyle (ed.) 1999, pp. 44–54.

Pyle, A. (ed.) (1999) *Key Philosophers in Conversation: The Cogito Interviews*. Routledge, New York.

Ramberg, B. (2015) Irony's Commitment: Rorty's *Contingency, Irony, and Solidarity*. *The European Legacy: Toward New Paradigms* 20/1, pp. 144–62.

Reid. J. (2014) *The Anti-Romantic: Hegel Against Ironic Romanticism*. Bloomsbury, London.

Rorty, R. (1972) The World Well Lost. *Journal of Philosophy* 69, pp. 649–65.

—— (1979) *Philosophy and the Mirror of Nature*. Princeton University Press, Princeton.

—— (1982) *Consequences of Pragmatism*. University of Minnesota Press, Minneapolis.

—— (1989) *Contingency, Irony, and Solidarity*. Cambridge University Press, Cambridge.

—— (1993) Putnam and the Relativist Menace. *Journal of Philosophy* 90/9, pp. 443–61.

—— (1997) What Do You Do When They Call You a "Relativist"? *Philosophy and Phenomenological Research* 57, pp. 173–7.

—— (1999) *Philosophy and Social Hope*. Penguin Books, London.

—— (1999a) Trotsky and the Wild Orchids. In Rorty 1999, pp. 3–20.

—— (2000) Response to Jürgen Habermas. In Brandom (ed.) 2000, pp. 56–64.

—— (2010) Reply to J. B. Schneewind. In Auxier and Hahn (eds.) 2010, pp. 506–8.

Rosen, S. (1967) *Plato's Symposium*. Yale University Press, New Haven.

Schneewind, J. B. (2010) Rorty on Utopia and Moral Philosophy. In Auxier and Hahn (eds.) 2010, pp. 479–505.

Schönbaumsfeld (2007) *A Confusion of the Spheres: Kierkegaard and Wittgenstein on Philosophy and Religion*. Oxford University Press, Oxford.

Sellars, W. (1997) *Empiricism and the Philosophy of Mind*. Harvard University Press, Cambridge, Mass.

Söderquist, K. B. (2013) *The Isolated Self*. Museum Tusculanum Press (Søren Kierkegaard Research Centre), Copenhagen.

Stewart, J. (2003) *Kierkegaard's Relation to Hegel Reconsidered*. Cambridge University Press, Cambridge.

Tessin, T. and Ruhr, M. V. D. (eds.) (1995) *Philosophy and the Grammar of Religious Belief*. Macmillan, London.

Tigerstedt, E. N. (1977) *Interpreting Plato*. Almquist and Wiksell, Uppsala.

Villa, D. (ed.) (2000) *The Cambridge Companion to Hannah Arendt*. Cambridge University Press, Cambridge.

Vlastos, G. (1956) *Plato's Protagoras*. The Library of Liberal Arts, New York.

—— (1991) *Socrates: Ironist and Moral Philosopher*. Cornell University Press, Ithaca.

Westphal, M. (1996) *Becoming a Self: A Reading of Kierkegaard's* Concluding Unscientific Postscript. Purdue University Press, West Lafayette, Indiana.

Whitehead, A. N. (1929) *The Aims of Education*. Free Press, New York.

Williams, G. W. (2012) Irony as the Birth of Kierkegaard's "Single Individual" and the Beginning of Politics. *Toronto Journal of Theology* 28/2, pp. 309–18.

Wittgenstein, L. (1961) *Tractatus Logico-Philosophicus*, trans. D. F. Pears and B. F. McGuinness. Routledge & Kegan Paul, London.

—— (2014) *Philosophical Investigations*, revised fourth edition. Wiley-Blackwell, Chichester.

Name Index

Agacinski, Sylviane, 145n14
Arendt, Hannah, 121–2, 153n20
Aristophanes, 11, 54, 80, 81
Aristotle, 49, 54, 56–7, 103, 136n7
Austin, John, 113, 118

Benjamin, Walter, 5, 6
Berlin, Isaiah, 51–2
Bernstein, Richard J., 103–4
Bloom, Harold, 130n28
Booth, Wayne C., 1, 3, 4–5, 6, 123–4
Brandom, Robert, 51, 128n20,
  133n44
Brooks, Cleanth, 1, 3–4
Burnyeat, Myles, 153n22

Cicero, Marcus Tullius, 6, 9, 37, 55,
  58, 59, 75, 120, 139n20
Climacus, Johannes, 11, 77, 93, 100,
  122, 148n31
  Cross on, 148n28
  ethical passion, 124
  illusion, 33
  "indirect communication," 36
  juxtaposition of concept and
    irony, 79

Lear on, 140n25
Lippitt on, 146n16, 147n26
revision of irony, 94–8, 121
truth, 78
see also Kierkegaard
Colebrook, Claire, 6
Conant, James, 127n9, 143n4,
  151n11
Cooper, John M., 135n6
Cross, Andrew, 90, 91, 140n27,
  148n28

de Man, Paul, 1, 3–5, 6, 144n7
Deleuze, Gilles, 6, 12
Derrida, Jacques, 6, 12, 70, 110,
  128n17
Descartes, René, 46, 51, 103–4,
  149n1
Dewey, John, 28–9, 45, 52, 116, 119,
  150n3, 152n15, 152n16, 152n17
Diamond, Cora, 126n1, 127n7,
  151n11

Fichte, Johann Gottlieb, 5, 88
Foucault, Michel, 6, 12, 63, 104,
  138n16

Subject Index